D0151966

Media Ethics
&
Accountability
Systems

Media Ethics

&
Accountability
Systems

Claude-Jean Bertrand

Transaction Publishers
New Brunswick (U.S.A.) and London (U.K.)

Library of Congress Catalog Number: 99-056519
ISBN: 1-56000-420-7
Printed in Canada

Library of Congress Cataloging-in-Publication Data

Bertrand, Claude Jean
  Media ethics and accountability systems / by Claude-Jean Bertrand.
    p. cm
  Includes bibliographical references.
  ISBN 1-56000-420-7
  1. Mass media—Moral and ethical aspects. I. Title.

P94 .B47 1999
175—dc21   99-056519

Contents

Introduction   1

Part 1: Basic Data

1. Major Distinctions   11
   Shackles on Press Freedom   11
   Press Regimes   12
   The Functions of Media   14
   Types of Media   16
   News and Entertainment   17
   The Participants   17
   Market, Law, and Ethics   20
   Morality, Media Ethics, and Quality Control   23

2. Principles and Values   25
   Nature and Effects of Media   25
   Human Values   29
   Freedom of Expression   31
   The Right to Communicate   32
   Media Values   35

Part 2: Media Ethics

3. Codes of Ethics : Types and Contents   41
   Nature of the Code   41
   Purpose of the Codes   42
   Who Writes the Codes?   42
   Brief History   44
   Categories of Clauses   44
   Codes for Entertainment Media   56
   Interpretation and Enforcement of Codes   59

4. Omissions   61
   To Know Oneself and to Master One's Field   61

Tradition, Conservatism, Routine   62
Single-Track Thinking   63
Fear of Novelty   63
Acquisition and Selection   64
Processing and Presentation   71
The Welfare of Society   73
The Entertainment Sector   74
Problems with Advertising   77

5. A Selection of Codes   79
   An International Declaration of
      the Rights and Obligations of Journalists   79
   The Code of Practice of
      the British Press Complaints Commission   81
   The Code of Professional Conduct of
      the Russian Journalist   86
   Third World Code from India: Norms of
      Journalistic Conduct   89
   Ouest-France Code
      for Reporting Crimes and Accidents   101

Part 3: Quality Control

6. The M*A*S Media Accountability Systems   107
   The Participants   108
   The Basic Means   111
   Written and Broadcast Documents   112
   Individuals and Groups   116
   Processes   121
   Two Special M*A*S   125
   European M*A*S 1998   129
   M*A*S in the French Press   133

7. Criticisms and Obstacles   137
   Criticisms   137
   The Obstacles   141

Conclusion   149
    A New Environment   149
    Quality Pays   150
    The Autonomy of Professionals   151
    Freedom and Quality   152
    Ethics Not Enough   152
    What Remains to be Done   153

Bibliography   157

Introduction

About a century ago, a huge scandal was exposed in France: the French had lent billions of dollars to the Czarist State and faced little probability of ever being reimbursed. At the time, "any resistance to new loans was fought down by the press, which, in cahoots with the banks, had grown used to a very profitable blackmail."[1] Much closer in time, in 1990, after the news director of a major French television network had allowed opponents of the government, in a country where the conglomerate that owned the network has big construction projects, on the air, the conglomerate president was heard to say: "She must become aware of the interests of a large industrial group like ours. If she doesn't, then the door is wide open: let her operate elsewhere." Such an incident may escape the public. What the public does notice is that the anchorman of the most watched newscast still held his job in 1999, eight years after it was revealed that he had fabricated an interview with Fidel Castro by inserting questions into a film shot during a press conference. And five years after he was involved in the investigation of a major crook for having accepted important gifts from him.

No wonder opinion polls show a distrust of media among the public and a willingness to let their freedom be curtailed;[2] less than a third of French people believe journalists are independent. "Americans are coming to the nearly unanimous conclusion that the press is biased, that powerful people and organizations can kill or steer news stories."[3] Everywhere, the various groups within the public express strong discontent towards the entertainment provided by the media.

---

1. In *L'Essor industriel et l'impérialisme colonial*, by M. Baumont, Paris, PUF, 1937 - p.196.
2. as shown by the annual survey published by the daily *La Croix* and the weekly *Télérama* since 1987.
3. Editorial on an ASNE (American Society of Newspaper Editors) newspaper credibility survey of 3 000 U.S. adults—in *Editor & Publisher*, December 28, 1998, p. 12.

Paradoxically, the media are accused of every sin at a time when they have never been better. To realize the progress, it is enough to flip through a few dailies from the nineteenth century, to glimpse a few television programs from the 1950s—or to read the diatribes of contemporary critics. The media are certainly better today, but still mediocre. And, mainly, while in the old days, most people could do without media, today, even in rural regions, the need is felt not just of media but of good media. Their improvement is not just a desirable change: the fate of mankind is predicated on it. Only democracy can insure the survival of human civilization and there can be no democracy without well-informed citizens and there cannot be such citizens without quality media.

Such a statement may seem exaggerated, but consider the former USSR where, between 1917 and the 1980s, hundreds of thousands of ancient books and works of art were destroyed; where vast regions were terminally polluted, where tens of millions of people were killed— because the soviet media could not, would not, expose and protest.

As the media do not fulfill their functions well enough, a crucial issue in any society can be summed up in one question: how can the media be improved?

Media

They should be considered all together as an industry, as a public service and as a political institution. Actually not all media enjoy that triple nature: for one thing, the new technology makes it possible for little mom-and-pop media to make a come back. Besides, a part of media products has nothing to do with public service, like supermarket tabloids, for instance. Lastly, many media, like reviews serving trades and professions, play no part in political life. Nevertheless, the media which enlightened citizens care about are the carriers of general news: those nowadays cannot shed any of the three combined features.

Conflict of Liberty

The result is a fundamental conflict between freedom of enterprise and freedom of speech. In the eyes of media entrepreneurs (and of advertisers), news and entertainment is a material with which to exploit a natural resource, consumers: and they strive to maintain a state of society which they find profitable. On the other hand, for citizens, news-and-entertainment is a tool they wish to use in their search for happiness, which they cannot attain without some changes in the status quo.

There is no easy way out of that dilemma. For many years, more than half the nations on earth did adopt one of two solutions. Both consist in eliminating one of the antagonists. Fascist dictatorships suppress freedom of speech, usually without touching ownership of media. Communist regimes suppress free enterprise and claim to maintain free speech. The effect is the same in both cases: the crippled media become a means to cretinize and indoctrinate.

One option might be to give total (political) freedom to the media industry. The termination of the State monopoly over European broadcasting, and of government control, has greatly improved democracy on the Old Continent and the development of media since the early 1980s. But the growing commercialism of media in the twentieth century and the concentration of ownership cannot very well coexist with media pluralism. "Conglomeratization" is not a favorable context for the needed independence of media. If freedom was total, the media would most probably prostitute themselves in both the news sector and the realm of entertainment. Europeans fear what they observe in the U.S., where nearly all media are commercial and regulation is minimal.[4] Eugene Roberts, the highly respected U.S. newspaper editor, deplores that "newspapers, with a few exceptions, concentrate on increasing profits to please share-holders."[5] In the U.S., a newspaper group can boast a 25 percent profit (Gannett)—while a television station can reach 50 percent.

The purpose of media cannot be just to make money. Nor just to be free: freedom is necessary but not sufficient. The goal for media is to serve all citizens well. Everywhere in the West, private media have for a long time enjoyed political freedom—yet they have quite often provided poor services. For instance, Britain's BBC is, constitutionally, less free than ABC in the U.S. but it has always served its listeners and viewers far better.[6]

---

4. see Ben Bagdikian, *The Media Monopoly*, Boston, Beacon, 1983 - 5th ed. 1997; and also Erik Barnouw & al., *Conglomerates and the Media*, New York, The New Press, 1997.
5. quoted in *Editor & Publisher*, 24/2/1996.
6. See Willian Baker & George Dessart, *Down the Tube: An Inside Account of the Failure of American Television*, New York, Basic Books, 1998.

So, should all media, on the contrary, be set under State control? The experience endured in the twentieth century of both communism and fascism has but reenforced the traditional distrust of people towards government. Quite rightly, they fear what could be a total manipulation of news and entertainment.

Clearly, total media freedom would be intolerable (can anyone be allowed to issue calls to murder or racial persecution?)—and media cannot be entrusted to the State. In every democracy in the world, there is agreement over the fact that media must be free but cannot be entirely free. The problem of balance between freedom and control is not a new one: John Adams, president of the U.S. from 1797 to 1801, wrote to a friend in 1815:

> "If ever there is to be an improvement in the fate of mankind, philosophers, theologians, lawmakers, politicians and moralists will find that the regulation of the press is the most difficult, most dangerous and most important they will have to solve." [7]

In Anglo-Saxon countries generally, too much confidence is lodged in "the market" as a guarantee of good media service—while in Latin countries too much trust is placed in the Law. Both are indispensable and dangerous. Without rejecting either, we need to find a supplementary instrument. That tool could be media ethics and accountability systems.

Media Ethics

It consists in a body of principles and rules, fashioned by the profession, preferably in cooperation with media users, in order that media can better serve most, if not all, groups within the population. Journalism is special among democratic institutions in that its status is not based on a social contract, a delegation of power by the people, either through an election or appointment dependent on degrees—or again through laws that would set norms of behavior for it. So to keep their prestige and independence, media need a deep awareness of their primary responsibility to provide a good public service.

Their ethics does not participate of legislation—or even of morality, in the narrow sense of the term. It is not a question of being honest or courteous but to assume a major social function. Certainly, quality

---

7.   Letter to John Lloyd dated 11 February 1815.

service is not easy to define, except in a negative way. What is excluded, for example, is limiting a regional daily to a bunch of zoned pages filled with little local events, as in the French provincial press—or again, for a big network, never devoting any of its programs to the education of children, as is the case in the U.S.

Of course, media ethics can only exist in a democracy. Whoever believes that humans are incapable of thinking independently, of running their own lives, cannot accept self-control. Auto-regulation can only be seriously considered in places that enjoy freedom of expression,[8] relatively prosperous media and competent journalists, proud of their job. In poor countries, there are few consumers, hence little advertising; so media are penniless, corrupt, or subsidized and controlled by the State. This implies that in many nations, even though they be officially democratic, media ethics is largely irrelevant.

Why Now?

There was a time when, at the mention of media ethics, media professionals would respond with scornful silence or some angry remark. Now more and more of them are developing an interest. They show it in books, in the editorials and articles of newspapers, in special issues of trade magazines, in broadcasts, symposiums, workshops. Why?

When the question is asked of European journalists,[9] their answers vary. They cite technological progress; concentration of ownership; the increasing commercialization of media; the mix of news and ads; the growing inaccuracy of the news; the Timisoara slaughter hoax[10] and the Gulf War; serious violations of professional morals by some reporters (invasions of privacy, especially in the popular press); a decline of the profession's credibility and prestige; the unjustified role of media in a political crisis; unacceptable links between media and government; the threat of legal restrictions on freedom of the press; an awakening of journalists' associations; a reaction to the laissez-faire of the 1980s; violence and reality-shows on television, etc.

---

8. Freedom House judged that in 1998 out of 186 nations, only 37% enjoyed press freedom.
9. From surveys I did in some 15 countries in 1993, 1994 and 1998.
10. In 1989, as the Rumanian dictator's regime was crumbling, Western reporters were fooled with a few hospital corpses into reporting a massacre by the secret police.

Factors of the Evolution

The main factors seem to number about half a dozen. First, the rise in the educational level of the public makes it more demanding and militant. More people understand how important good media services are; how unsuited to the modern world is the traditional concept of news. And media consumers are now realizing that they can and should do something about it.

Journalists are far better educated too. It seems that more of them wish to fulfill their functions satisfactorily and to enjoy greater social prestige. In that quest, the majority finds it unacceptable to suffer from the ethical misbehavior of a minority.

The mediocrity of media hurts even those who are to blame for it. Nearly everywhere, proprietors lament the decline of newspaper sales and of the time spent watching the major networks. Also the advertisers rightly worry about the credibility of the media in which they place their ads. Moreover, for a number of years, business people in general have shown more concern for the impact of the products they put on the market. More realize now that quality, that is to say public service, does pay.[11]

Both the bad and the good effects of technology have helped media ethics. It makes media more democratic because more numerous and less expensive. At the same time, it causes distortion: the reporter on the scene talks directly to the viewer, with no pause to analyze. And the manipulation of information is made easier, the falsification of pictures especially.

And then, of course, there is the Web. In January 1998, for the first time, it was discovered to be a news medium—when Matt Drudge launched the Clinton-Lewinsky scandal in cyberspace. Everyone can access Internet, which is wonderfully democratic. On the other hand, anybody can dump anything there. So the need will grow, ceaselessly, for honest screeners, for journalists that can be trusted, who are competent and accountable.

The growing profit-orientation of media makes them more sensitive to public opinion but it multiplies the reasons they have to distort the news and to vulgarize entertainment— and to mix the two. Highly visible is the proliferation of the professional persuaders: admen/press officers/media consultants/experts in electoral campaigning.

---

11. See James O'Toole, *Vanguard Management*, Garden City (NJ), Doubleday, 1985

Lastly, the collapse of the Soviet Union contributed to the change. By putting an end to the myth of a State solution to media problems, it revitalized ethics, the only acceptable strategy against exploitation of media by economic forces. Also, media ethics had suffered from being sometimes associated with communist propaganda, filled as the latter was with noble denunciations (of racism, of colonialism) and purple patches (about world peace or economic development)—which were echoed by the governments of "non-aligned" nations and, in democratic nations, relayed by various marxist academics.

Nowadays, ethics suffers mainly from not being known and understood by the general public, of course, but also, more surprisingly, in media circles.

General Structure

In the present book, first a few basic distinctions are made that are needed to clarify the atmosphere around the debate. Then comes an exposition of the principles on which media ethics is founded. Then comes a systematic presentation of the many clauses contained in codes of ethics. After that catalogue of rules, a chapter is devoted to what, very regrettably, is not to be found in codes—and is not often mentioned. The next chapter surveys the various nongovernmental means of inciting media to respect ethical rules. And the last chapter deals with the many obstacles and criticisms met by those accountability systems.

PART 1

Basic Data

1

Major Distinctions

Media ethics is a misty zone. And the guides to the area often are philosophers using obscure language and having no experience as practitioners. Or, conversely, they are practitioners with little knowledge of what the thinking has been in the field. Some mix up the concepts while others wrap worn-out clichés in jargon. The result is confusion, sterile disputes, and inaction. So it seems useful at the start to establish a few clear distinctions.

Shackles on Press Freedom

One can be held responsible only for acts committed voluntarily. So ethics can develop only when media are free. Their freedom to inform faces five major obstacles, that are quite different from each other. The oldest, the technological one, is fading away. The second shackle is political: from its beginning, the development of the press was curbed by the crown and its courts; today, even in democracies, the government still strives to censor or distort the news. The third threat, which has grown more dangerous throughout the twentieth century, is economic: the use of media solely to make money. The fourth obstacle may come as a surprise for it is rarely mentioned: it is the conservatism of media professionals, their outdated ideas and methods (see p. 62). The last obstacle, never mentioned, resides in the surrounding culture, in traditions such as the status of women in moslem nations, tribal loyalty in Africa, respect for the old in Japan. The guilty party there, in other words, is the public.

Press Regimes

Basically, there are four possible regimes,[1] two that are democratic and two that are not. Each is based on a concept of the universe and of mankind. Put simply, pessimists regard the human being as a brute and deny him/her any free will: he/she needs to be watched, restrained, indoctrinated. On the other hand, optimists look upon humans as rational creatures: if they are given access to information and left free to exchange ideas, then they are able to manage the society in which they live.

The Authoritarian Regime

This type was the most common until the mid-nineteenth century. In the twentieth century the fascist State took over where absolute monarchies had left off. In such a regime, usually, media remain private firms run for profit, but the powers-that-be closely control contents. News and entertainment can be subversive. Ideas being broadcast must meet the needs of the ruling clique. No opposition press is permitted: nor any political debate. Even some types of human interest stories are forbidden, as they can be interpreted as signs of social dysfunction.

The Communist Regime

There media do not exist independently from a totalitarian State which has absorbed all institutions and industries: media operate like cogs in a gigantic machine. A concept like press freedom is irrelevant. That regime, inaugurated in Russia at the beginning of the 1920s was extended over Eastern Europe after 1945 then to China after 1949 and, in the 1960s to a large part of the Third World.

In the totalitarian regime, the State uses its media to broadcast its instructions, to persuade people to follow them and to teach the official ideology.[2] The first function of media is to lie, to hide whatever does not serve the interests of the ruling *nomenklatura*. By the end of

---

1. See F. Siebert, Th. Peterson & W. Schramm, *Four Theories of the Press*, Urbana, University of Illinois Press, 1956. And, from the same publisher,   J.C. Nerone ed., *Last Rights: Revisiting "Four Theories of the Press,"* 1995.
2. Article 1 of the Chinese press code : journalists must "be loyal to their country and to communism and apply the principles and policies defined by the Party ".

the twentieth century, that regime seemed on the way to extinction: it had proved contrary to economic development, to social welfare, to the expansion of knowledge, to world peace—and, of course, to political democracy. That, however, leaves much of the marxist criticism made of capitalist media unaffected.

In the Third World, it used to be claimed that media had a special part to play: to serve development, to educate the population, to weld different ethnic groups into a nation and to preserve the local culture. Actually most often, in military dictatorships calling themselves socialistic, the undeveloped media were used to keep a despot in power and to serve an urban elite.

The Liberal Regime

The liberal, or libertarian, regime became the international norm thanks to Article 19 of the United Nations' International Declaration of Human Rights (1948). It is founded on a doctrine born in eighteenth-century Europe, in the Age of Enlightenment: all events must be reported and all opinions put on the "marketplace of ideas." Then human beings can discern the truth and use it to determine their behavior. If the State does not interfere, all will go well.

That beautiful illusion did not resist the growing commercialization of the press from the turn of the twentieth century. Whatever was profitable was then deemed to be good. Moreover, as corporations have a natural tendency to concentration, there was a risk that the power to inform, the privilege of setting the topics of the national debate, could fall into the hands of a few irresponsible media owners, which, at the end of the century, seemed to be happening.

The Social Responsibility Regime

That concept, born of a more realistic perception of human nature, is an extension of the previous one. The notion was launched in the U.S. by the "Commission on Freedom of the Press,"[3] made up of eminent personalities from outside the media sphere. The media greeted its report, *A Free and Responsible Press* (1947), with indifference or rage. But over the next twenty years, the ideas it presented were generally accepted.

---

3.   chaired by R.M. Hutchins, president of the University of Chicago.

According to that doctrine, it is better that media be not owned by the State or even controlled by it. On the other hand, media are not ordinary commercial firms whose success can be measured by profits. It is normal that they should seek profitability but they must be responsible towards the various social groups, i.e., respond to their needs and wishes.

If citizens are displeased by the service they get, then the media must react. Better it is that they amend themselves but if they do not, then it is necessary and legitimate that Parliament intervene. Experience shows that very often it is to avoid such an intervention that media develop a concern for ethics.

Keep in mind that those four press regimes never exist in a pure state. In authoritarian regimes, citizens have always had access to some underground or transborder media. And in liberal democracies, even in the U.S., a consensus exists among citizens that media need to be regulated in the general interest.

The Functions of Media

To judge whether media serve the public well, you need to know what services they are supposed to provide. These fall into about six categories. To each function corresponds a dysfunction, which is the target of media ethics.

To Watch the Environment

In present-day society, only the media are capable of providing us with a quick and full report on events taking place all around us. Their role is to obtain the information, to filter it, to interpret it, and then to circulate it. In particular, they must keep an eye on the three political powers (executive, legislative, and judiciary) in the interval between elections.

To Insure Social Communication

It is necessary, in a democratic community, that compromises be reached through discussion, that a minimal consensus be established without which there can be no peaceful coexistence. Nowadays, the forum where most of the discussion takes place is the media.

They relate every individual to a group, fashion the groups into a nation, contribute to international cooperation. Besides, small media insure lateral communication between people who share the same ethnic origin or a profession or some passion—but who, in mass society, are often scattered far and wide.

To Provide an Image of the World

Nobody has a direct knowledge of the whole planet. Beyond the range of one's experience, what one knows comes from the schools or from conversations, but mainly from media. For the ordinary person, the areas, the people, the topics that media do not mention, do not exist.

To Transmit the Culture

The cultural legacy of any group needs to be handed over from one generation to the next: a certain vision of the past, the present, and the future of the world, an amalgam of traditions and values that give an individual an ethnic identity. Everybody needs to be told what is and is not done, what should be thought and not thought. In that socializing process, Churches in most of the West no longer play the part they used to play, especially in Europe. Nor does the family, especially in the U.S. There remain the schools—and the media which influence individuals during their whole lives.

To Contribute to Happiness: To Entertain

In mass society, entertainment is more indispensable than before to lessen the tensions that can lead to sickness, physical or mental. It is mainly provided by media. The user of media expects entertainment from them more than anything else—and that function combines very well with the other five.

To Sell

Media are major vehicles of advertising. Their owners' primary purpose, quite often, is to seduce a public so as to sell it to advertisers. They try and create a favorable environment for the ads. For some observers, advertising plays a positive part: it informs and, by stimulating consumption and competition, it lowers prices (including those of media). Critics, on the contrary, accuse it of manipulating people, of causing waste and pollution.

Types of Media

A (mass) medium is an industrial firm which, by specific technical means, broadcasts, most often simultaneously, the same message to a large group of scattered individuals. This definition does not include the telephone, opinion polls and universal suffrage. Mail and billboards can be excluded as their messages are rarely other than commercial. Recordings are primarily material used by radio. As for the cinema, it has become not so much a medium as a provider of the small TV screen through cable, satellites, and cassettes. In common usage, media are newspapers, magazines, radio and television.

Within that definition, media are so different that ethics cannot be exactly the same for each. The distinction is clear between the printed press and audiovisual media; or between "public" media (under State control[4]) and commercial media and noncommercial private media.

However, a fundamental distinction to be made is between the press that deals with general information and the opinion press. Codes of ethics concern the former which, to a large extent nowadays, is politically neutral. It is accepted that the latter—whether religious, ethnic, political—can, for ideological reasons, distort reality,[5] blackout opposite ideas, be unfair, or even insulting. But it should not lie or encourage to violence or racial hatred. Such a press most needs that press freedom be protected, since it usually irritates some part of the population and often the powers-that-be.

The specialized press stands apart. Its contents largely come from freelance contributors whose ethics are difficult to check, and most of its revenues come from specialized advertisers. Lastly, the controlled-circulation press is pure advertising—and the in-house reviews published by commercial or public institutions partake of "public relations."

---

4. Europeans distinguish clearly between the permanent non-partisan "State" and the elected "government" that happens to run the nation at a given time.
5. The Kansas code (1910) considered that a partisan publication was not a newspaper.

News and Entertainment

Entertainment media belong in a special sphere. For some of them which deal with pure amusement (like crossword magazines), ethics is irrelevant. However, the public expresses innumerable grievances towards most other such media—while ethicists seem to be strictly focused on journalism. Since media entertainment is produced by a huge industry[6] and does not seem to have a political role, the trend has been not to bother about its ethics. In most countries, a few laws, regulations (about pornography, for instance), and contractual pledges are judged to be enough. Yet in the mid-1990s the public (with politicians following it) has expressed strong disapproval of the hysterical violence on the small and big screens and of the vulgar sensationalism on radio.

The boundary between journalism and entertainment has never been clear and it is growing less so: the popular press has always favored entertainment and now most commercial media glaze most of their products with it. Some overlap is inevitable, admittedly: a news story can be interesting yet unimportant; conversely, much can be learned from entertainment. Both types of media provide knowledge and education—and it is indispensable that they both serve the public well. But there should be no confusion of their domains. Their goals differ: accurate and useful news on the one hand and, on the other, amusement that hurts neither individuals nor society. Rules of behavior can hardly be the same.

The Participants

Employers and Employees

The media and the people who work for them should not be treated as one entity, as is often done in the U.S. Their responsibilities are different. Journalists are quite capable on their own of committing many professional sins. Nevertheless, the editorial policy of a medium, and its attitude towards ethics, are determined by the proprietors and their agents.[7]

---

6. Until 1952, the U.S. cinema was not protected by the First Amendment: the justification was that movies were mere commercial entertainment.
7. even though it happens that in small media a person will be both owner and reporter.

Top executives are expected to possess business talents, not a moral conscience. And they are expected to respect laws and regulations: if they don't, they have to answer for it in court.[8] Actually, nowadays, quite a few of the managers are nothing but employees, responsible to shareholders, who themselves are only interested in the bottom line. However, because these people have power, anyone concerned with media ethics had better not trigger their hostility.

As for journalists, they used to be nothing but docile mercenary scribblers, with the exception of a few great pens. Nowadays, their craft draws close to a profession. Specialized university training in journalism has developed in all advanced democracies, as well as professional associations and codes of ethics. As "professionals," their number one purpose must be to serve their clients well.

One category of journalists form a separate class and a very important one: the editors, appointed by management, who have by delegation both the right to set editorial policy and to hire and fire. The part those professionals play in ethical matters is crucial because they can use punishment to enforce the rules. It is to be regretted that they use it very discreetly: dirty linen is not washed publicly.

The Rank-and-file and the Stars

The media user often tends to confuse those two groups. Ordinary newspeople are numerous, not very well paid, exposed to multiple pressures, sometimes despised by news sources—and they are accused of most of the ills affecting the media. In relative obscurity, they labor hard to inform as well as possible. Overworked, insufficiently equipped and seconded, they stumble sometimes or skid off the road—and the accumulation of such minor failings forms an impressive heap.

The stars of journalism, mainly television performers, are few in number, extremely well paid,[9] and famous. Inevitably, they serve as models both in the eyes of other newspeople, mainly the younger ones, and in the eyes of the public. They are at far greater risk of violating ethics: temptation is rife and celebrity can go to one's head.

---

8. Nevertheless, some owners will subsidize a quality medium to acquire prestige and influence. Roy Thomson did it for the London *Times* in the 1960s, and was made a lord.

9. By using their fame in different media, like a TV commentator also doing a daily radio show and a column in a newspaper and a weekly TV magazine. In the U.S., thanks also to lecture tours (with presentations paid up to $ 60 000); in France, by emceeing trade conferences or even the inauguration of a shopping mall.

The faults they commit, sometimes very serious and dramatic, cause serious harm to the whole profession.

The Advertisers

They are the more important customers of most media and they insure their prosperity. They are concerned with the quality of contents inasmuch as it generates an aura of credibility favorable to the advertising message—and enables some of them to reach very attractive audiences. On the other hand, they lean on media in various ways to obtain a blurring of the border between ads and news. So they are sometimes called the worst opponents of "social responsibility."

Media Users

Social communication is too important to be left to the sole professionals. Anyway, freedom of speech and of the press is not a prerogative of theirs: it belongs to the general public. Now polls show it clearly: the public feels it is being duped, exploited by the media. Its animosity is sometimes justified but not always. Too many people are not aware of the technical requirements of the press and express unfair grievances. Also, "news" often means abnormal tidings, usually unpleasant—and the public cannot resist the ancient inclination to kill the messenger bringing bad news.

Apathetic or unorganized, ignorant or intolerant, media consumers sometimes form an obstacle to freedom of the press and often show little willingness to defend it. In France, for instance, in the days when the Minister of Information had direct control over television, did citizens start a boycott of the annual users' fee? Were there any petitions signed against the sale of the major public TV network to a tycoon of the construction industry, in the 1980s? Were there any street marches in Australia against the concentration of 60 percent of the daily press in the hands of a multinational conglomerate? Anywhere in the world, were there demonstrations against the portrayal of women as morons in advertising?

Whether it is indifferent or hostile, for good or bad reasons, the attitude of the public is politically dangerous. For the survival of democracy, a remedy needs to be found. It seems that one was slowly developed along the twentieth century: to make the media "socially responsible."

Market, Law, and Ethics

The Market

The long experience of the Soviet Union and of its satellites has proved it: free enterprise is necessary to freedom of information and discussion. That was clear in most European nations when television was entirely dependent on the State. Actually, it is the absence of competition which causes the mediocrity of media. That was obvious in the U.S. before the blooming of cable and satellite television, when three identical commercial networks monopolized the airwaves. How can we accept that a bunch of firms grab a vital public service and exploit it just to make money? How can we accept their claim that the institution of the press must be totally free, that all regulation must be eliminated?

The "market" cannot suffice to guarantee good social communication. At best, it makes it possible for a majority to express itself. At worst, the media become servants to a wealthy minority, on the one hand; and on the other hand, they broadcast to an undifferentiated mass what seems to displease it least. In the days of jungle capitalism, in the second half of the nineteenth century, the Gilded Age in the U.S., it was demonstrated that in the absence of State regulation, the business caste cares little for public service, in other words, for ethics.

The Law

Consequently, laws are needed to force the media to provide adequate service to all publics. By law is meant acts of parliament, rules edicted by regulatory agencies, court decisions, and contractual promises made by firms so as to obtain licenses. Enforcing those obligations belongs to the police, the magistrates and regulating commissions, like the FCC in the U.S. or its French equivalent the CSA.[10]

Democratic law intervenes to proscribe certain practices, all the rest being permitted. If everyone agrees that some measure is in the public interest, why not make it into a law, against libel for instance or against incitement to murder? Advertising for cigarettes is forbidden on television in many countries. But the law is not restricted to prohibiting: most European countries give their citizens a legal "right to

---

10. Conseil national de l'audiovisuel. A major difference is that the CSA does not deal with telecommunications.

reply" in the press. Many use State subsidies to help small newspapers survive despite the trend towards concentration. Europeans tend to fear business interference rather more than that of government.

The law is not restrictive by nature. It can help the media do their job. The Swedish press law grants newspeople an exceptional series of guarantees: there can be no censorship, even in time of war; journalists cannot be asked about their sources; everyone has access to official archives (with a few exceptions); media get very special protection if ever they are taken to court.[11] The judiciary power, especially when it is independent, can encourage the media to assume their functions fully—and can interpret restrictive laws to their advantage. The European court of human rights has confirmed to British journalists that they have a right to protect their sources, which was denied to them by British courts.

The U.S. attitude seems absurd: American newspeople refuse any press law (and almost all means to enforce ethical rules) but rarely utter a word of protest against the great commercial restrictions to their freedom—or about laws that are favorable to the status quo and profitmaking.

Law and Ethics: the two fields are not clearly separate. Admittedly, you seldom find, in Western codes, prohibitions that are normally contained in laws (e.g., that national security must not be jeopardized) or often are legal (e.g., that editorial matter be distinguishable from ads[12]). Yet codes cite duties of journalists that can be included in the law in all other countries or some.

The right of reply is legal in France, but not in Great Britain or the Netherlands. The German code recommends that the names and pictures of under age delinquents be not published—which the law prohibits in other countries. In the U.S., the CBS network demands that opinion poll results be accompanied by methodological data: that in France is a legal obligation.

Obviously, some acts are condemned both by law and ethics. And many codes demand some rights for newspeople which enlightened legislation grants them elsewhere: professional secrecy in Germany; access to archives in the U.S.; the right to refuse assignments contrary to one's deep held principles, in France. Laws and regulations set up a

---

11. Like a trial by jury (not a normal institution in Scandinavia) and the possibility for the judge to ignore the jury if it finds against the media, which he/she cannot do if the jury finds for the media.
12. The Norwegian code recommends it. In France, the law demands it.

framework within which each practitioner has some latitude to opt among several behaviors. Media ethics establishes another, stricter framework but still leaves a choice, which is made by every individual according to his/her personal values.

Media can cause serious harm without violating the law. Acts permitted by law can be contrary to professional ethics, like for a journalist to accept an industrialist's invitation to a luxurious vacation. Conversely, ethics may tolerate illegal acts, like stealing a document to prove a scandal which seriously impairs the general interest.

Although there are overlaps, the two fields are distinct and it is important that they remain so. Using laws to decide press matters is always dangerous. There are many reasons for that: a law is only as efficient as the sociopolitical environment[13] allows it to be. It can be variously used by the government of the day, in a lax or in a muzzling manner. Some fields (like privacy) are so ill-defined that a law, which is either too vague or too precise, can do more harm than good. Some social attitudes (towards sex, for instance) change so fast that the law can petrify a soon-to-be outdated norm. Lastly, quite a few offenses involve no breaking of the law. A court can punish an act committed by media but can hardly do anything about an omission. Besides, the juridical machine is slow, expensive, and intimidating.

There are cases when neither the law, nor the market, nor ethics can do anything. The disgusting "Radio Mille collines," which in Rwanda incited Hutus to genocide the Tutsis, could only have been suppressed by military force.

Journalism as a Profession?

Might the solution come from a Council of pundits, set up by the State but independent from it? "I have always regretted that there was no Order of journalists whose function would be to defend the freedom of the profession and the duties which that freedom necessarily involves" said Albert Camus.[14] It is clearly better for the press to exert self-discipline, within reasonable limits. That ideal conforms with the wish of some newspeople that journalism be admitted among the professions, together with law and medicine.

---

13. Sanctions based on the 1881 French press law have become rare and light. The law needs to be updated and regenerated but legislators fear to antagonize media people.
14. in *Le Monde*, 17/12/1957.

But journalism is not a profession. For various reasons. First, it is not based on a science (consisting of a global theory and an organized body of knowledge): in almost all countries, a journalist is not compelled to hold university degrees, or pass tests, proving the acquisition of a store of learning. And a journalist does not need a license to practice. Rarely is he/she self-employed.[15] Besides, as there is no direct relationship between practitioner and client, the State has not felt the need to protect the citizen from the journalist by forcing rules upon news media. Or by creating special courts. There are no Orders of journalists, except in a few Latin nations like Italy where it suffers from having originated in the days of Mussolini. Anyhow, the existing Orders of physicians or lawyers do not strike one as being very efficient.

Considering the function of political watchdog and protester that some of the media must assume, most newspeople and outside observers reckon that media ethics should keep away from the State.

Morality, Media Ethics, and Quality Control

Morality

The distinction between those three notions (whatever the name given each of them) is needed and too often is not made. "Morality" is just another term for the "personal ethics" of an individual, a sense of duty based on a vision of the world and an experience of life. For some critics, like J.C. Merrill,[16] that intimate sense of what is right and wrong is the only permissible restriction to the freedom of the journalist.

Media Ethics

Latins call it "déontologie" (French) or "deontologia" (Italian, Spanish).[17] It applies within a profession. Often it is an unwritten tradition

---

15. It should be noted, however, that in hospitals also, many doctors are wage-earners, as are lawyers employed by big corporations.
16. John C. Merrill., *The Imperative of Freedom: A Philosophy of Journalistic Autonomy*, New York, Hastings House, 1974.
17. The word exists in English. According to the *Oxford English Dictionary*, it was first used in 1826. Its quote is from Jeremy Bentham: "Ethics has received the more expressive name of deontology".

which determines by consensus what "is done" and "is not done," what behavior is admissible and what behavior will get a practitioner ostracized by his/her peers. In most countries, associations of reporters and editors have found it useful to draft a charter of professional duties, even though some journalists fiercely criticize that usage (see p.137).

Quality Control

For some people, the terms "morality" and "ethics" have unpleasant connotations. They remind them of sermons, philosophy classes, Boy Scouts, and even the "moral order" in totalitarian regimes. Mainly, they seem irrelevant in a world where media are becoming ever more commercial because of ever fiercer competition.

"Quality Control" is a concept little used up to now in the media world. Its advantage is to be wide: it covers personal ethics, media ethics, and any initiative on the part of management to serve the public better. Its major attraction is that it is neutral and can satisfy all protagonists in social communication. For media users, it means good service. For journalists, it implies a better product, higher credibility, increased prestige. For owners, it calls to mind the Japanese commercial success, hence bigger profits. Lastly it rhymes with action, not talk.

2

Principles and Values

Nature and Effects of Media

Media are part of the very complex social system of modern societies and of its many sub-systems. The whole operates as a vast living organism. Each element depends on the others. One deficient sub-system can cause the entire machine not to function properly. So, even in a liberal regime, the autonomy of media is limited. To a large degree, they are and they do what the past dictates, what the culture, what the economy of the country demands, what decision-makers want, what consumers and citizens desire.

Besides, one must take into account the triple nature of the media, especially when dealing with ethics. Being altogether an industry, a public service and a political institution gives them an ambiguous status from which most problems derive.

Public Service

Even in parts of the world where the press does not enjoy guarantees by the Constitution (as in the U.S.) or a general press law (as in France), tradition endows it with privileges that set it among major public services. The media hold those legal or traditional rights on behalf of citizens. That delegation of power has no explicit contractual basis: in order to keep it, the news media need to deserve it, by providing high-quality services.

25

It was in the U.S. between the two world wars that some people started giving serious thought to media ethics,[1] at the same time when an interest developed in professionalism and college education in journalism. In 1947, the Hutchins Commission published its report. In the 1960s, more and more attention was given to the "social responsibility" of media.[2] That is the preferred term in the U.S.: it implies that journalists must render accounts to the people. In Europe, the favorite term is "public service." Unfortunately, that term is associated with the State because for many years the State managed, or strictly regulated, most public services. But in fact, the two phrases describe similar realities, which others call media ethics or quality control.

A Political Institution

Contrary to the three others, the Fourth Estate is in the hands of persons that have been neither elected nor appointed for their competence: undeniably, this seems contrary to democratic principle. A phrase of Stanley Baldwin,[3] Tory Prime Minister of Britain in the 1920s and 1930s, has become famous: what the proprietors of the (conservative) popular press were "aiming at," he said, "is power, and power without responsibility—the prerogative of the harlot throughout the ages." The media can avoid that kind of denunciation by finding means of being accountable.

Thus will they have a better chance of retaining their freedom. This is always threatened because itself is a threat for the authorities. On the political Right as on the Left, in all nations, whoever possesses some power seeks to limit media freedom. The two self-proclaimed champions of libertarianism, Margaret Thatcher and Ronald Reagan (interestingly nicknamed the Great Communicator) attacked press freedom more than any of their predecessors. Ethics is the best protection. "Freedom will be the better safeguarded when the personnel of the Press and of all other media of information constantly and voluntarily strive to maintain the highest sense of responsibility."[4]

---

1. E.g. *The Ethics of Journalism* by Nelson A. Crawford (1924) or *The Conscience of the Newspaper*, by Leon N. Flint (1925).
2. See, among others, William Rivers, W. Schramm & al., *Responsibilities in Mass Communication*, New York, Harper & Row, 1957, 3rd ed. 1980.
3. Actually coined by his relative Rudyard Kipling (1931).
4. Quote from the UNO draft of an international code of ethics .

An Industry

When mass communication appeared, it made possible, for the first time in history, that every citizen participate in the management of his/her country at every level. But it required that media adopt an industrial structure, hence, in Western countries at the beginning of the twentieth century, a capitalist organization. Today, a very large part of the media belong to big businesses whose primary goal is not public service.

For Milton Friedman, the famous U.S. economist, "the one and only social responsibility of business is to increase its profits." More precisely, a leader of the *Wall Street Journal*[5] stated: a newspaper is "a private enterprise, owing nothing to the public, which grants it no franchise. It is therefore affected with no public interest. It is emphatically the property of its owner, who is selling a manufactured product at his own risk."

But the expenses of the media industry have regularly increased as unions obtained fairer salaries and as technical progress made greater investments necessary. Media firms have naturally tried to eliminate competition and to concentrate—and thereby reduce costs.

Certainly, media can serve the public all the better as they have bigger financial resources. But public interest may be jeopardized. When media are absorbed into conglomerates, a vast political power is lodged with a few people whose major purpose is not to inform the public. Those people, who are not accountable to anyone but the shareholders, meaning actually the big financial institutions, have the power to decide what happened in the world by deciding whether it shall be reported. It is always regrettable when, in a country, some sector of the economy falls under the control of a monopoly or oligopoly. What if that happens to media, which are one of the nervous systems of society?

The Effects of Media

Who would question that the functions of media in the modern world are important? And as media are often credited with immense power, they are often held responsible for all the ills of present-day society, by the Left and the Right, North and South, by the powerful and the humble, by the young and by the old.

---

5.   January 20, 1925.

One principle is unquestionable: media produce effects. What effect they may have on children is one of the issues most studied in the social sciences. And doubt no longer exists: depending on their contents, and circumstances, media produce good or bad effects. Generally speaking, there is agreement that they can exert a strong influence, in the long term, if the message is homogeneous and mainly if they push in the direction users want to go.

However, in Europe, even today, the media are held to be all-powerful, an elitist tradition that was reenforced by Marxist criticism, and also by owners and journalists who derive various gratifications from such a belief. Quite a few people are convinced that if a message is published, it will certainly have an impact, like a bullet on a target. "Critics look at the press and see Superman when it's really just Clark Kent," wrote Michael Schudson.[6] This partly explains the undue importance taken by contents analysis and semiotics.

One thing is often forgotten, even in the U.S.: for a message to exist, there have to be two persons, a sender and a receiver. Now it has been abundantly demonstrated that a media consumer is no passive receptacle[7]: he/she interprets the message according to his/her personal experience, environment, needs, and desires. He/she is no victim of the media, but a user. Consequently, the main influence of media is by omission: what they do not say is more influential than what they do say.

Media, undoubtedly, do have an important effect also by supplying information, by choosing what events, what people are worth noting. Sometimes just the publication of a piece of news triggers action by government even before citizens react. Undoubtedly, media set the agenda for society. As the common phrase goes, they cannot dictate what to think, but what to think about. Or not to think about: media can generate what Elisabeth Noelle-Neumann has called "the spiral of silence": events, people, ideas thus disappear from the public consciousness. That said, on issues that matter for them, people fashion their own opinions—and conversely the opinion of the majority can dictate the attitude of media (especially the commercial ones).

No evidence of the citizens' autonomy and of their resistance to media, is as spectacular as that provided by the former Soviet Union

---

6.   In *The Power of News*, Cambridge, Harvard UP, 1995 - p. 17.
7.   Striking in 1998 was the U.S. public's refusal over a period of a year to adopt the media's views on the Clinton-Lewinsky scandal.

and its satellites. According to the late marxist concept, capitalist media were but a superstructure used by an economic elite to enslave the masses. Actually, it was the Sovietized media, truly enslaved, that could not do their job. In the late 1980s, the citizens peacefully overturned those totalitarian regimes.

This should be an encouragement to those who count on media users to demand and obtain that media be ethical, control their quality, give good service.

Human Values

Rights and duties are inseparable. But the human being is inclined to claim rights without mentioning the duties coupled with them, especially nowadays, especially in the West. Well, media ethics is mainly concerned with duties. It posits that freedom and responsibility go hand-in-hand. Like any religion or philosophy, it has developed rules that fix limits to individual freedom and prescribe obligations to each of us. Those rules emanate from a body of moral principles. A given person subscribes to certain principles because they correspond to the vision he/she has of fellow human beings and of the universe. And they correspond to his/her ideas about society and its institutions, which themselves depend on the knowledge and experience the person has of them.

Fundamental Values

If a single value exists on which all humans can agree (except a few fanatics), it is the survival of the species,[8] the fate of the planet. That concern should move all of us, whatever our ideology, whether or not we have a religious faith. The human race is threatened as it has never been before. Humans have found the enemy: it is themselves. All must feel responsible about it. Fortunately, a majority shares certain values on which social morality is founded: respect for human life, a concern not to hurt anyone needlessly, the promotion of justice and human rights, the improvement of the fate of others, democracy.

That we can talk of universal values is a consequence of the globalization started in the nineteenth century or earlier, at the Renais-

---

8. See Hans Jonas, *Das Prinzip Verantwortung*, Frankfurt/Main, Insel, 1979.

sance. But even today there are values which some traditional cultures do not accept, like the equality of women, tolerance towards different human beings, privacy, universal suffrage. On the credit side, some of those same cultures do not tolerate the frantic selfishness in the social jungle of the West. Moreover, each culture has specific features, quite independent of its stage of economic development: thus female nudity offends in Saudi Arabia and in the U.S., whereas in Europe it has become a normal part of the seaside landscape and of advertising.

The Judeo-Greek Legacy

In most industrialized democracies, the ideology traces its origins to the beginning of Christianity: its roots are Jewish and Greek. In a nutshell, the human being was formed in the image of God but was defiled by original sin. Noble and corrupt, he/she possesses rights but has been burdened with duties. Two traditions coexist within Western civilization, stressing one or the other natures of man, the fallen angel or the creature of God: the Catholic and the Protestant, Latin and Anglo-American, Southern European and Northern European. The former, more authoritarian, insists on group solidarity and social stability. The latter, more libertarian, stresses individualism and enterprise. Within the latter was born modern democracy and industrial civilization. Among its values that are now spreading all over the globe: the equality of all human beings, a faith in human progress, respect for the law, for the contract that binds society.

To guide humans in their behavior, great moral precepts have been formulated over the centuries. Thus Aristotle recommends always to follow a via media between opposite excesses. Kant believes that deep in every man exists a moral sense, the determination to do what is right: according to this "categorical imperative," a moral act is one that can be generalized. As for John Stuart Mill, the utilitarian, one should always seek the greatest good for the greatest number.

Democracy

Nowadays, a majority of mankind seems convinced that the people should dictate their will to the government and not vice versa. Democracy, which some claim is essentially Christian, and even Protestant, may seem incompatible with traditional Islam, according to which politics is in the hands of God, whose will is interpreted by the wise.

Incompatible also with Buddhism, Confucianism, Hinduism, or tribalism. Absolute allegiance to an ethnic group, or respect for castes to
insure social stability, or loyalty towards ancestors, elders, clan chiefs:
all such values do seem contrary to democracy. Actually, India is the
largest democratic country in the world and Japan one of the two most
powerful.[9] When you look closer, you find, for instance, that Confucius
held two values to be fundamental: concern for others and fairness.
You find that Confucianism, based as it is on respect for order and
hierarchy, is also based on devotion to the community, cooperation,
and courtesy.

Freedom of Expression

All the nations of the world proclaim as an ideal that each of their
citizens must enjoy "human rights." In practice, the individual possesses none of them if he/she does not have one of them: the right to
know. All rights have to be won and then defended, ceaselessly. You
cannot wage that fight without being informed.

Press Freedom

The first mission of the media professional, whatever his/her other
functions, is to use the freedom to communicate in order to inform
people of his/her observations of the surrounding world. That freedom
is one of the few (so-called) "absolute" human rights that correspond
to a vital need. Without communication, there can be no human society, hence no extended survival of the species.

When a dictatorship is set up, whether lay or theocratic, monarchi-
cal or imperial, military or colonial, bourgeois or proletarian, it
always suppresses freedom of speech and freedom of the press.
So that freedom has become as much a sign as a factor of democracy.
It is worth repeating that while there can be no true freedom
without limitations, there can be no responsibility without freedom.
The media professional needs to be free both from State interference
and from proprietor's interference. He/she also needs "economic" freedom: without a decent salary, a journalist will find it hard to resist
corruption.

---

9.   Admittedly, the Asian concept of democracy is not identical to the Western one.

Positive Freedom

"Everyone has the right to freedom of opinion and expression; this right includes freedom to hold opinions without interference and to seek, receive and impart information and ideas through any media and regardless of frontiers": such is Article 19 of the International Declaration of Human Rights adopted by the UNO in 1948.

Late-nineteenth-century technology and later electronics have caused a tremendous expansion of media, which, in its turn, has required a conceptual revolution. For many years, "freedom of the press" was conceived as a right of every citizen. And it truly existed, after political censorship ended, so long as a small sum was enough to launch a periodical. Then, as costs escalated, that freedom became negative: among several newspapers offered for sale, the citizen could reject those that did not answer his/her needs or showed the world in a light he/she disliked. Since 1945 at least, in most cities, the number of newspapers has been reduced to one. Launching a new daily requires millions of dollars. Consequently, "freedom of the press" has become no longer a right of the citizen but the privilege of plutocrats and governments. That is why a new concept has emerged.

It first appeared in Anglo-Saxon and Scandinavian democracies. There one finds a consensus on national values, the custom that major political parties alternate in power and, as regards the news media, a tradition of freedom and reasonable aggressiveness. In other words, nations where the opposition, partisan or journalistic, is well integrated in political life.

Press freedom started being defined not simply as the absence of censorship, political or other, but as the affirmation of a task to be achieved: satisfying each citizen's right to information. His/her right to be well informed. And the right to inform, i.e., to have some access to the media.

The Right to Communicate

Freedom of speech and of the press cannot remain a mere non-prohibition, which benefits only a small minority.[10] It needs to turn into a right to communicate, for all. For U.S. law professor Jerome

---

10. "Freedom of the press is guaranteed to those who own one", was the way the U.S. media critic A.J. Liebling put it (*The New Yorker*, May 14, 1960).

Barron, the ban on all government censorship (contained in the First Amendment of the U.S. Constitution) implies the existence of a right of access for all citizens: what is the point of having the freedom to express oneself if one cannot get heard? Decreeing an access to media is almost[11] unthinkable. Media ethics is a respectable way of obtaining it.

Communication being an essential need of human beings, a "right to communicate"[12] is called for: the right for individuals, groups, and nations to exchange any message by whatever channel. Therefore the obligation for the community to provide the means of the exchange. If there were no school, the right to education would not mean much, or the right to vote if there were no elections.

What For?

Is it reasonable to want to change into a "positive" freedom a "negative" freedom that took centuries of struggle to acquire—and which has not yet been extended to the whole planet? There are four major reasons. First, technology in recent years, especially the Internet, has made global communication possible, easy, and inexpensive. Mankind is leaving the short era of the mass media in which the dearth of communication channels and the cost of investments forced upon us one-way communication, the over-concentration of message-sending power and, in the electronic field, a close control by the State. Now we enter the cyber age.

Second cause: mass society. The average individual has at his/her disposal more education, more money, and more time than ever. In developed countries, for most inhabitants, science and welfare programs are dispelling the specter of destitution and early death. Yet human beings feel adrift in the "lonely crowd." They feel powerless against private and public bureaucracies. More than ever, they feel the need to be integrated in a community, to take part in the running of their own lives. Evidence of that appears in the fights waged by ethnic minorities, women, consumers, or environmentalists. Also, more than before, people feel their dependence on the rest of the world. For those many reasons, people feel the need to inform and be informed.

---

11. In the U.S., cable channels have been set aside for public access. In France, radio channels are set aside for non-profit associations.
12. The concept was launched in 1969 by the Frenchman Jean d'Arcy, picked up in the 70s in Canada and the U.S., then by the International Institute of Communications and UNESCO.

Third cause: the new awareness that information is an essential natural resource, a very precious one, on which peace and prosperity depend. An awareness that on its free and plentiful circulation are predicated the emancipation of the individual, economic development, the solution of social problems, and a smooth adaptation to the accelerating changes in the environment.

A fourth cause may reside in a feeling of solidarity which is slowly spreading to the globe, in spite of great cultural differences and economic inequalities. The greatly increased exchanges of products, culture, and (mainly) information appear as the one means to avoid an economic, ecological, or nuclear disaster.

Insufficient Communication

Social communication operates at different levels and in various directions. On the international level, a powerful nation or business corporation (like Radio France Internationale or a Hollywood studio) addresses a weak nation. A weak nation addresses a powerful nation. Or another weak nation. Intergroup communication goes vertically from top to bottom: from government to people (e.g., through a State radio) or from firm to general public (e.g., via a national daily). Or from bottom to top, as by polling or referendum. But it can also be lateral, from one group to the other (e.g., the public access channel on a local cable system).

In three directions it seems that the right to communicate is not used much and should be used more: from weak to powerful nation, from citizens to powers-that-be, and from group to group within the mass. One purpose of media ethics is to remove the obstacles to that communication.

Except one. There is a perfectly admissible barrier to communication: in case of a refusal to communicate. At the individual level, it is considered unobjectionable if someone will not buy a newspaper or switch on the radio. But it does seem a little strange that some people request the right not to be assaulted by advertising. At the international level, some nations (like the U.S.) do not take it well that other nations want to protect their cultures by limiting the importation of foreign audiovisual products. Actually, everywhere you hear people demand balanced two-way communication—except in the U.S., of course, because of its hegemony on media markets.

Media Values

Dealing with media ethics means talking about the duties of journalists. Those duties imply that media people possess rights, both as human beings and as practitioners of a particular job. The law often secures some of those rights for them—and some codes mention them. The right to a decent salary; the right to be acquainted with the editorial policy and consulted before any major change in management; the right to refuse an assignment incompatible with ethics or personal beliefs; the right of access to information, etc. Acting as agents of the public, they go where masses of citizens cannot go, do things the public cannot do: they enjoy privileges, but they must be accountable.

Human Duties

A journalist's obligations consist, first of all, of the duties of any human being, as applied to media. They must respond to instinctive needs that all humans seem to feel: even as a child, we wish to express ourselves freely; and we want grown-ups to be truthful and be responsible. In Moses' Ten Commandments, six at least are applicable to social communication: 2. no worship of idols, no perjury or blasphemy; 5. respect for elders, for traditions; 6. no violence; 7. no pornography; 8. no corruption; 9. no lying; 10. solidarity with other journalists. Similarly, the fundamental values in the Gospel, once summarized by a French Catholic daily in five words: freedom, dignity, justice, peace, love—are poles around which all the clauses in journalistic codes of ethics could be clustered.

The Western Legacy

Journalism was born and developed between the Renaissance and the French Revolution in a Western Europe imbued with the values of the Reformation, especially individualism, individual responsibility, work within a calling, moral strictness. But imbued also with the rational and liberal values of the Enlightenment. And later, with the concepts of "laissez-faire," of utilitarianism and "social Darwinism."

The great thinkers of previous centuries never dealt with mass media as they appeared only at the turn of the twentieth century, but those who knew the press in the eighteenth century did not have much esteem for it. More recently, the authors of ethics codes, interested in practice and ignorant of philosophy, have rarely bothered to decode the works of abstruse thinkers.

From the eighteenth century, with the progress of sciences and technology, an ideal of professionalism started developing. Prestige and power were expected to derive, no longer from an ancestry or from land ownership, but from the competence and the social useful-ness of an individual. Then, from the end of the nineteenth century, media professionals created associations to set their own rules for entry and for practice, with the aim of getting their independence acknowledged by the State and their worth recognized by the public. Specialized schools were opened. Codes were written.

Universal Values

Media values are largely the same in all regions of the globe where the regime is democratic. Media ethics is founded on universal values, like the refusal of hatred, of violence, of the contempt for human beings (fascism) or just some types of them (racism). Media ethics is in harmony with most ideologies, Judaism, Buddhism, Confucianism, Christianity (Catholic and Protestant), moderate Islam, humanism, so-cial democracy. But it does not agree with extremisms, totalitarian-ism, or fundamentalisms.

Of course, the hierarchy of values varies from one culture to the next. Thus, a university study of U.S. and Chinese newspeople has shown that both groups believe that the information released must be accurate and complete, but the former places aggressiveness and in-quisitiveness on the front rank of journalistic virtues—whereas the latter ranks humility and loyalty first.

What constitutes a profession, according to Deni Elliott, are values shared by most of its members, even when they are not set down in writing. In the case of journalists: to publish a full, correct, relevant, balanced report on the news; to give citizens the information they need; and, as they do so, not to cause anyone any harm. To put oneself in the shoes of the people affected by the published article; to consider the possible effects, immediate and long term, of what is being re-vealed. More generally, journalistic values are, obviously, related to the functions of media. Hence the necessity that the reporter be clearly aware of those functions (see p. 14).

Medical Values

On the occasion of a 1994 conference, which gathered a dozen trade associations, the medical profession in Great Britain reiterated its values, ancient but still valid for the twenty-first century. What is remarkable is that they would just as well suit the media profession: commitment, compassion, integrity, competence, spirit of inquiry, confidentiality, responsibility, and advocacy. Physicians, too, worry about the declining confidence their clients have in them, about the lodging by them of complaints and malpractice suits. They consider that the whole profession must feel responsible for the actions of its members and must organize its self-discipline. They recommend peer evaluations with the participation of patients. They judge that the profession must actively take part in the betterment of society.

Part 2

Media Ethics

3

Codes of Ethics: Types and Contents

Most nations where the political regime is not dictatorial now possess at least one code of press ethics. From Norway to South Africa, from Japan to Turkey, from Canada to Chile. It is diversely called a code of honor, of conduct, of practice or (in Latin countries) of "deontology"—or again, canons of journalism, a charter of journalists, a statement of principles, a declaration of the duties and rights of journalists, etc.

Nature of the Code

At the time when a code is adopted, usually there already are laws relative to the media. But the drafters of the code realize how insufficient and dangerous they are. What they write is not a sacred text to which they would expect every journalist to swear absolute loyalty— but a guide which can only become operative if the journalist is endowed with a moral sense.

In every field of activity, some things "are done" and some "are not done."[1] Traditionally you learn which is which on the job and whoever violates a rule runs the risk of being ostracized in the workplace. But to stay alive, a tradition needs to be discussed, cleansed, updated, structured—and set down on paper, locally or nationally. Otherwise, it remains too hazy, sometimes ambiguous, or even quite dishonorable.[2]

---

1. Codes sometimes allude to some spectacular ethical violation that took place soon before its drafting.
2. It was long tolerated that journalists receive an "envelope" after the press conferences of corporate leaders. The French press even now is far more tolerant of freebies and junkets than the U.S. press.

41

Besides, in parallel to the national tradition, in most media organs, there are editorial principles which are transmitted orally or published, even sometimes for distribution to the public or the advertisers.

Purpose of the Codes

In every organized craft (real estate for instance, or pharmacy), the ethics code aims at eliminating crooks and quacks. The code informs the public on the particular trade: it tells it about its rules of conduct. By thus increasing its credibility, it insures the loyalty of its patrons and, in the case of media, the loyalty also of its advertisers, the source of its prosperity.

The code protects the customer, but what it does, too, is generate solidarity within the group and preserve the prestige of the profession, hence its influence. Those who adopt the code not always have the intention or possibility of respecting the rules, but they thus post the Tables of the Law. They give themselves an ideal. And they strive to reinforce the moral conscience of every professional by making clear the values and principles unanimously recognized by the profession. The code can provide a feeling of security, of collective strength.

In addition, the code aims at avoiding State intervention. The latter can be dreadful in the case of media. When the media cause the public to distrust them, then legislators draft, and sometimes pass, repressive laws. Whenever such a danger looms, it triggers gestures of self-reform among professionals, the first of which is to draft a code.

The charter, especially if it also contains a list of the rights of journalists, can be a useful restraint on management; this is why quite often media-owners refuse to endorse it, as in France. Thanks to it, professionals acquire a protection against an employer that would request them to act contrary to the public interest: they can argue that such behavior would cause them to be rejected by their peers.

Who Writes the Codes?

"Codes" issued by a government are not considered here: they are nothing but executive orders. Among true codes, some are national, adopted by one or several professional associations (owners and journalists in Ghana, for instance). Some are international codes like that of the International Federation of Journalists (FIJ—IFJ). Others have been issued by associations of media owners (like the "charter of proper behavior" by the French Society of Provincial Daily Newspaper Owners (SPQR), or by unions (as in Switzerland and Britain), or again by associations of newspeople (like the U.S. Society of Professional Journalists—SDX). Some codes concern only one medium, like the ASNE code for the print media or the former code of the NAB for broadcasting in the U.S.[3] Some codes are specific to a publication, like that of the daily *La Suisse* (in Geneva) or of the *Chicago Tribune*, or again to a broadcasting network, like NHK in Japan.

A code of professional ethics should normally be conceived by the professionals themselves. That is why some of them refuse to take into account the regulations prescribed by employers for their employees,[4] like the "editorial charter" of the French daily *Nord-Éclair*—or again the stylebooks, such as that of the Associated Press, that include instructions to newspeople (from punctuation to punctuality) and ethical rules.

The objection of some journalists to such "corporate charters" or "codes of conduct" seems unsound to me: they consist of rules that are no different, only sometimes more concrete, more precise. Most often, such codes were drafted by the top editors, true journalists, in cooperation with the staff. The twin advantages of those books of rules is that they can be included in hiring contracts and that they carry sanctions. Besides, some widely accepted national codes were developed jointly by journalists and media owners within some institution to which both parties belong, like the press council for the German Pressekodex. The codes, by the way, can be supplemented by the decisions and declarations of media councils.

When professionals get down to composing a code, they had better invite some of the external experts that observe and analyze the behavior and contents of media. And also invite media users, to whom, after all, the freedom of the press belongs. It is well that a code be accepted by all the members of a profession. It is better that it be also accepted by the surrounding society.

---

3. ASNE: American Society of Newspaper Editors. NAB: National Association of Broadcasters.
4. In 1976, U.S. newspapers obtained the right to decree a code for their staff. Now many of them have.

Brief History

Codes started multiplying at the beginning of the twentieth century, partly an effect of the progressive movement which denounced the evils of jungle capitalism, especially in the press. Then also journalists became conscious of forming a separate caste.

In 1896, Polish journalists in Galicia gave themselves a list of duties and a court of honor. In 1910, a press association in Kansas adopted a code which applied to both publishers and editors. In 1924, over half a dozen U.S. dailies had their own codes. The first national code was French: the "Charte des devoirs" of the SNJ union of journalists— adopted in 1918. As for the first international code, it came in 1926 from the InterAmerican Press Association. Then in 1939, the International Federation of Journalists (FIJ) published its Code of honor.

Codes emerged everywhere after the second World War. From its birth, the United Nations tackled the issue. But its project of a code, sent for evaluation to some 500 press-related associations in 1950, was never adopted, mainly because professional organizations refused, quite rightly, that government bodies (like the members of the UNO) stick their noses in media affairs.

The next wave of interest for media ethics swelled at the turn of the 1970s, within UNESCO, the Council of Europe, the FIJ, the International Press Institute—after the great protest demonstrations of the sixties everywhere. The fourth wave was raised by Gulf War coverage (1991) and other contemporary scandals.

Categories of Clauses

It is to be expected that the definition of "media misbehavior" vary depending on the culture of a nation, its economic stage of development, its political regime. It cannot be the same in a communist and in a liberal country, in an archaic and a hypermodern country, in a Moslem and a Hindu country. However, in most codes, the same fundamental rules are to be found. The explanation is the community of culture in the influential nations where the first codes appeared—and also international dialogue over several decades.

Among media professionals, academic observers, consumer advocates, there is no deep disagreement about what media should and should not do. Of course, the very numerous codes differ, if only because of their length. The SNJ charter covers half a page, as compared to the sixty-five pages of the code of the Louisville (Kentucky) *Courier-Journal*. And every code omits some clause or other—but one gets the feeling that if some major item is missing, the probable cause is a wish to keep the code very short or mere forgetfulness.

Synthetic Code

Fundamental Values
- to respect life
- to promote solidarity among human beings

Fundamental Prohibitions
- not to lie
- not to appropriate someone else's property
- not to hurt anyone needlessly

Journalistic Principles
- to be competent (hence self-confident, capable of admitting errors)
- to be independent, from political, economic, intellectual forces
- to do nothing that may decrease the public's trust in media
- to have a wide and deep definition of news (not just the obvious, the interesting, the superficial)
- to give a full, accurate, fair, understandable report of the news
- to serve all groups (rich/poor, young/old, conservative/ liberal, etc.)
- to defend and promote human rights and democracy
- to work towards an improvement of society.

Quite often, the recommendations in codes are thrown in higgledy-piggledy. Even some experts, when they undertake a comparative study of codes, quickly slide into confusion. To give a clear idea of media ethics as a whole, one needs to introduce some order. For the following analysis, a wide crop of rules was gathered from international, national, in-house codes—after which the rules were distributed into seven categories. To avoid repetitions, each clause is quoted but once, with a few exceptions. So the rules cited in a given category must be regarded merely as a sample.

According to the Nature of Rules

Ideal Rules. It is well that a goal be set towards which professionals should strive although it is often obviously impossible that they reach it: never to accept an assignment contrary to ethics; always to know the topics well with which they deal; leave their own opinions out of any report they give; always give several viewpoints; ceaselessly fight for human rights.

General Rules. Some rules are valid for every citizen always, without exceptions (or very few). Some actually have been formalized into laws, or religious precepts: not to lie, not to steal, not to cause pain to anybody needlessly. Other rules are specifically meant for journalists: not to falsify a piece of news; not to accept financial advantages or other gifts from people wishing to secure, or to stop, the publication of some story; not even to give the impression of behaving unethically.

Rules with Exceptions. Sometimes the end justifies the means. Some rules can be ignored by a medium when it is in the public interest, especially if the news story exposes serious antisocial behavior or threats to public health. The reporter must not hide his/her identity from sources, or secretly obtain information (with a hidden camera, for example), or incite anyone to break the law, or intrude uselessly into the privacy of people—except, of course, when the Defense Minister of his country shares a call-girl with the naval attaché of a hostile nation.[5]

Controversial Rules. Naturally, journalists will differ on the answers to ethical questions, especially on certain issues. Should media question whatever comes from the government, as in the U.S., or should they abstain from "unjustified" attacks on institutions and elected or appointed officials (Korea, Turkey)? Are editors-in-chief accountable for the acts of their journalists (Britain, Sweden) or should the journalist never pass the buck to someone higher in the hierarchy (France)? Should the journalist never express his/her opinion (Japan) or is he/she entitled to express it (Egypt)—an old disagreement between France and the U.S.?

Other points of controversy may be mentioned. In Spain, it is normal not to reveal one's sources: politicians like to make off-the-record statements—whereas in the U.S., it is (or was?) considered a sin not to indicate a source. Can a reporter let a source have a look at his/her story or broadcast before publication? Answers differ: in no circumstances; only to check facts. In any case, if access is granted, the

---

5.   The Profumo case, Great Britain, 1963.

reader/listener/viewer should be told. In Sweden, it is agreed that sexual crimes should not be mentioned except if there a risk for the public; on the contrary, in the U.S., many want to lift the taboo, which is said to harm the victims.

According to Media Functions

Watch the Environment. As most codes concern journalism, naturally most clauses fall into this category. A journalist should not yield to any pressure aiming to influence the choice or presentation of news, whether the pressure is internal or external. Further, some codes give him/her the mission to demand that public affairs be truly public, such as official archives, meetings of representative assemblies, decisions by the executive.

Give an Image of the World. As most of what we know about the planet, outside our personal experience, comes from the media, the journalist should make sure that we get a correct picture, that his/her story will not increase xenophobia, racism, or sexism, etc. He/she must improve the image traditionally given of other peoples in his/her own country (by avoiding stereotypes, for instance) and he/she must generate curiosity and sympathy for other cultures.

Serve as a Forum. It is through media that social communication operates, which is needed for the indispensable compromises to be reached, in a given community. On major public issues, various viewpoints must be given. The Lithuanian code requires that the whole gamut of opinions be presented. The many social groups must be able to express themselves or at least to reply if they are incriminated. And to do it openly: in Latvia, in the mid-1990s, after an electoral campaign, the press itself revealed that all parties had bought favorable stories from most media.

Transmit Culture/Entertain. Those two functions are assumed mainly by entertainment media, which are presented separately (see p.56).

Sell. For a long time, media have been accused of prostituting themselves.[6] Some sections especially are suspected of corruption, those devoted to restaurant reviews, tourism, fashion, beauty, and automobile. The same applies to magazines that live almost exclusively

---

6. When Upton Sinclair thrashed the press in 1919, he entitled the book *The Brass Check*, from the token used in Wild West brothels.

on advertising from a narrow sector of the economy. So codes are clear: there should be no suppression or distortion or invention to please advertisers. They should be given no favor, whether that means publishing releases on the occasion of the inauguration of a store, a new car model, a fashion presentation, or a new show (Sweden). And a journalist must have no activity whatsoever that is related to advertising or public relations.

According to the Scope of the Rules

Rules Specific to Particular Media. Most codes focus on print journalism. It would be good if, as in Japan, all media, dailies, public broadcasting, commercial broadcasting, magazines, the recording industry, book publishing, had codes. There are few codes specific to broadcasting, except in the U.S. It seems the explanation is that despite deregulation in the 1980s, those media remain more controlled by law than print.

Radio and television journalists, with their bulky equipment, should intervene as discreetly as possible so as not to distort the event they are covering (march, trial). Unintentionally, they sometimes kindle demonstrations and/or violence. The viewer should be warned before a scene is aired that it might upset him/her; and when stock shots are used or some event has been reconstituted. The face and voice of any person who might suffer from being identified should be masked.

Rules Concerning One Aspect of the News. Some categories of professionals adopt specific rules for themselves: financial reporters, investigative journalists, Catholic newspeople, sports reporters, or press photographers. Generally, their codes expand and particularize clauses that exist in ordinary codes.

However, there are three areas often covered by general assignment reporters that have attracted special attention: terrorism, crime, and trials. Some big media have set instructions concerning the attitude to adopt in case of urban riots: be discreet, cold, very careful with rumors. Avoid live reports, never obstruct the action of police.

In "human interest stories,"[7] no feature of the accused should be mentioned (race, religion, profession, etc.) that is not relevant to the

---

7. Denmark has a code limited to the reporting of crimes. The French daily *Ouest-France* has one restricted to "human interest stories" (see p. 00).

case; the reporter should not reveal the names of minors accused of crimes; not recall past offenses, especially if they have been amnestied—not to mention the right to pardon for criminals who have served their sentence. The names of relatives or friends of anyone accused of a crime should not be given, unless there is a serious reason to do so. Victims of crime or people accidentally involved should not be placed at risk of being hurt: for instance, by making it possible for confederates of an arrested criminal to locate them. A journalist should always remind the reader/listener/viewer that no one is guilty until proven so by a judge and jury.

Every citizen has a right to a fair trial, without the court being influenced by the press. Strict British laws drastically limit reports of trials. But in many nations, such rules are left to ethics. A journalist must explain legal terms. And not publish anything that might affect the opinion of the court.

Rules Specific to Some Countries. They depend on the environment of a nation, on its inherited culture, or economic development, or media system. During the Cold War, the Austrian code recommended prudence when mentioning people living in totalitarian countries.[8] Scandinavian nations are very much attached to human rights: with exceptions justified by public interest, media there should not publish photographs without a caption giving the names of people in it, should not mention suicides, not even reveal the names of the accused before a court has reached a verdict. Anglo-Saxon countries, being puritanical, have a fixation on matters pertaining to sex.

In Japan, the Confucian tradition stresses social harmony, loyalty to the group, the respect of hierarchies and of elders. Journalism is far less aggressive, iconoclastic than in the U.S.

Some clauses characterized "socialist" codes that were nothing but propaganda, like public access to media, the defense of human rights, multiculturalism, educational media, a New World Information Order, the struggle for peace and against colonialism. They also characterized some documents sponsored by UNESCO at a time when it was accused of yielding a little too much to Third World and Soviet pressure. This is no sufficient reason to reject them: some are excellent. A Finnish expert regards the pre-1991 Soviet and Hungarian codes as among

---

8. Austria had common borders with the Soviet empire and many of its citizens had relatives behind the Iron Curtain.

the most complete, together with that of Finland.[9] The rules edicted by the oft-vilified press tycoon W.R. Hearst are also remarkable.

In Moslem countries, ethics is closely linked to religion. Within certain élites, it is influenced by Western "'modernism'"—but most regimes being authoritarian, hence hostile to press freedom, media ethics is irrelevant. If there is a "code," it is official.

Too much should not be made of those differences between codes in various countries. Most are differences in degree or have to do with minor issues. They should not dissuade the profession from seeking an international agreement on media ethics which would help journalists defend their rights.

Third World Rules. There are regions of the world that face problems which have (almost) disappeared from industrialized democracies— and where media ethics usually consists in governmental regulation. There you find a concern to preserve the nation, usually of recent birth. A journalist should respect the State and its agents, not assail institutions, never jeopardize national security,[10] by reporting matters that could breed dissatisfaction in the armed forces, for instance.

The codes request that media strengthen national feeling, that they not foster conflicts between ethnic or religious communities, that they fight fanaticism and tribalism. Actually, in practical ethics, in Nigeria, for instance, tribalism is central: is considered good and fair whatever serves your own ethnic group. The same goes for castes in India.[11] Codes recommend to be careful in the report of events (e.g., murders, riots) that could inspire imitation. That concern for social harmony is not unanimously approved, of course: in the eyes of some, it aims at conserving an unfair social order, an oppressive political regime, an archaic vision of the world.

Media must mobilize energies for development; actively serve national interests and goals, the education of the masses, social justice, economic progress. Cultural life must be decolonized. Media must in no way be controlled by foreign capitalism—nor should a journalist ever accept any subsidy from it. Such are some other points made in Third World codes.

---

9. Pauli Juusela, *Journalistic Codes of Ethics in the CSCE Countries*, Tampere, University of Tampere, 1991
10. It is interesting that U.S. media often are criticized on those points.
11. See Cooper (1989). p. 124s. (Nigeria) et 147s. (India).

According to the Category of Professionals

Many rules concern both journalists and media owners. Editors are both journalists and agents of management. In small media, the owner may also be the principal reporter. In some nations (like Sweden), the two categories have signed the code. Both, for instance, are asked not to distort the news for reasons personal (ambition, vendetta), ideological or financial.

Rules for Owners (and their agents) Only. In the codes, the duties of "media" are rarely mentioned, for at least two reasons: first, the law often dictates them; second, many codes were drafted by associations of journalists for their own members. The attention media owners pay to ethics varies from one country to another: very weak in the U.S. and strong in Nordic countries. Yet it would be useful if they set an example and it is necessary that they allow their employees to follow it. First, by paying salaries that insure their dignity and honesty: in India, in Russia, in Latin America, many journalists cannot survive on their wages. Also owners must not assign tasks that might hurt the reputation of the profession—or place their employees at risk of injury without adequate compensation.

The media manager should strictly separate journalistic and business interests. He/she must not omit certain news, or give others undue importance, to pursue political, advertising, or demagogic interests—or to protect the interests of his/her group or of business in general. More precisely, he/she should not automatically insert every press release or any ad; or promise advertisers any editorial support for their ads. And even less should he/she give great coverage to an event or an association in exchange for advance purchase of a large number of copies. Lastly, he/she must feel responsible that the contents of advertising be tasteful, accurate, and reasonably harmless.

Rules for Journalists Only. Quite a few codes specify that newspeople must keep neutral. Among other things, they should not take part in demonstrations and sign petitions. Mainly, the professional must remain scrupulously honest: avoid any conflict of interest by refusing any moral or material favor, presents, discounts, services, free trips, free tickets, part-time employment (lectures, emceeing conferences). Neither should he/she accept money in the shape of prizes awarded by non-media institutions. More generally, he/she should not use his/her status as a journalist to obtain any kind of personal advantage, e.g., in return for clandestine advertising. *A fortiori*, as some codes feel the need to specify, a newsperson should not sell his/her pen, practice blackmail or extortion. In the Russia of the 1990s, it was commonplace for a businessman or a politician to buy himself an interview.

Financial journalists form a special case. They must not draw any personal advantage from the information they gather before it is published. Nor should they endeavor to use their articles to push the value of stocks up or down and thus obtain illicit profit. Many media require that they disclose to management the contents of their personal portfolios.

A professional should not even give the impression that he/she might be corrupt. It is very regrettable that at the end of the twentieth century, a former chairman of the French equivalent of the National Association of Manufacturers felt he could say that "journalists, they can be bought with canapés or with envelopes."

According to the Type of Accountability

One is not just "accountable": you are accountable to some one. A media professional is accountable first to himself/herself. He/she should not betray his/her convictions, must refuse any assignment contrary to ethics. He/she is also accountable towards his/her employer. A journalist must respect the law, must not publicize the internal affairs of his/her company, or in any other way hurt its reputation. Neither his/her private life, political commitments, or huge honoraria for outside jobs should generate suspicion of a conflict of interest. Even less should he/she work without permission for other employers, especially competitors—not to speak of "creative writing" on an expense account—or a resume. However, a journalist is mainly responsible towards the four following groups.

Towards Peers. Journalists should not in any way discredit the profession. They must fight for journalistic rights, against all censorship, and for access to information, public and private. They must behave fraternally towards other journalists: not cause them harm for selfish purposes; not offer to work at a lower salary than what they get; not appropriate ideas, data or products belonging to them. They must help colleagues in trouble, especially foreign correspondents. In 1991, French forces took part in Desert Storm, yet the French wire service AFP was excluded from the pools formed by U.S. media—and when AFP later sued, a U.S. court rejected its complaint.

Towards Sources. A journalist should respect embargoes on news releases; should be careful about the accuracy of reported words (especially if published within quotation marks); should not distort a statement by quoting it out of context, or summarizing a long declaration. No item should be published that was given on condition it be kept as background; or a source be revealed to whom secrecy had been promised—unless, as always, public welfare demands it. Conversely, a journalist must always keep his/her critical sense awake: not let himself/herself be manipulated or misinformed; and be wary of statements by witnesses under shock, or weak-minded persons.

Towards People Involved in the News. A journalist should not cast charges, even though they be true, if they do not serve the public welfare. If someone is accused or criticized, that person must be given the opportunity to respond. The journalist should not mention any characteristic of a person that is not relevant, like gender, name, nationality, religion, ethnic group, caste, language, political orientation, job, address, sexual preference, mental or physical handicap. And even less should he/she utilize that feature to discredit the person. No uselessly derogatory terms should be used, nor insinuations. Generally, unless the public interest is at stake, the right to inform must never be exerted in a way that may harm individuals or groups, physically, morally, intellectually, culturally, or economically. For instance, the publication of pictures of horrible accidents or crimes can hurt the relatives and friends of the victims.

Towards Media Users. In no case should a professional cause loss or injury to consumers, whether by using "subliminal" methods to put through an audiovisual message, or by publishing sensational reports on medical or pharmaceutical discoveries likely to generate unjustified fears or hopes.

Media also have duties towards the community where they operate: they must not offend the moral conscience of the public; they must identify the needs of all groups and serve them. Moreover, media have duties towards society as a whole. Merely abiding by the laws is not enough. They must look after the interests of the public instead of satisfying its curiosity; publish nothing that can severely harm the family institution; not sing the praises of jungle law; fight against injustice and speak on behalf of the under-privileged; improve cooperation between peoples; not speculate on fear; not cultivate immorality, indecency or vulgarity; not encourage the lower instincts, like greed or violence; not glorify war, violence or crime.

According to the Phase of Work

Obtaining Information. First rule, obvious: information should not be invented. But neither should dishonest means be used to obtain a news item or photograph—like hiding one's identity, trespassing on private property, setting up an ambush with lights, cameras, and mikes, secretly recording a conversation, stealing a document—unless that is justified by public interest and no other means will succeed. Also, the journalist should mention the fact in the story.

The 25-part report published by the *Chicago Sun-Times* in 1977 after it operated a bar, the Mirage, equipped with recording equipment, so as to expose the corruption of various municipal services, caused a vast cleansing operation but did not win the Pulitzer prize: some believed there had been entrapment, incitement to commit a crime.

Information should not be bought from the witnesses of crimes or from criminals. Nor should compulsive means (lies, harassment,[12] threats, blackmail) be used. Some codes say that children should not be interviewed on affairs concerning them. The privacy of people should not be invaded, especially that of humble folk, especially when they are struck by some misfortune. The naiveté of people unaccustomed to dealing with media should not be abused; and they should not be ridiculed. Any interviewee should be warned of the use that will be made of his/her statements—but should not be informed of the questions in advance.

Selection. No quickie sidewalk interviews of the man-in-the-street and similar worthless documents should be published. Rumors should be set aside, as well as unchecked stories and press releases—or should be tagged for what they are. An hypothesis should not be published as if it was a proven fact, nor a piece of news, even if true, if it has no social usefulness and can hurt the people involved.

No information (facts or words) should be omitted through laziness (when research or processing is called for) or through cowardice (in the case of an unofficial source or when a news item has not been mentioned by any "big" media). Or because of undue pressure, internal (e.g., from the business department) or external (e.g., from advertiser or source), direct or indirect.

---

12. The fatal accident of Princess Diana in 1997 put the spotlight on the paparazzi, reporter-photographers who hound celebrities of all kinds. But they normally serve gossip magazines, which belong to the sphere of entertainment .

News should be selected because of its importance, its usefulness to the public—and not because of the curiosity of an undereducated mass public, its thirst for fun and games, its voyeurism. Space should not be inordinately wasted on titillating news (sex, crime) or news likely to demoralize the population.

Processing/Presentation. Advertising should be made clearly distinct from editorial matter. News and views should not be confused—though any medium can be partisan if it wishes to be, provided information is not distorted. In order for a full and understandable report on the news to be provided, events should be set in context and be accompanied by analysis and comments. Opinions should be based on correct facts and be clearly marked for what they are. In the case of controversial issues, several viewpoints should be given. Whole pages or broadcast programs should be devoted to all important issues.

Data should be meticulously checked since a correction cannot always repair the harm done by publication of a mistaken report. If sources cannot be indicated, then the reason should be given. Headlines and subheads should correspond to the contents of stories, as should summaries of them. Letters-to-the-Editor should not be distorted by editing: cuts should be marked. Photos can be wrongly interpreted: precautions should be taken to avoid it. Photos, audio tapes, video tapes should not be processed in such a way as to cause distortion. Rehearsed photos should be labeled as such.

No piece of news should be given undue importance, be sensationalized (by excessive language, dramatic photos) especially if violence is involved. Uselessly shocking descriptions should be avoided, especially in the case of executions, accidents, acts of cruelty, which might traumatize children.

Post-publication. In France and Latin countries, a right of reply is granted by law. In Anglo-Saxon countries, such an obligation causes outrage, but U.S. codes abundantly recommend that editors voluntarily offer that possibility. Also, a medium must acknowledge its errors, fast and visibly.[13] If some complaint is made, an investigation should be initiated and, if it finds cause, correction and apologies should be published.

During the Gulf War, most of the figures given by U.S. military sources were inaccurate: e.g., 547,000 Iraqi soldiers before the con-

---

13. Despite its reputation for arrogance, the *New York Times* at least once (July 13, 1987) published a two column wide correction on the front page, over the fold.

flict—but only 183,000 after; Patriot missiles destroying not nearly all Scuds, but only one in ten. Usual war propaganda, but in the aftermath very few dailies or TV news-teams admitted the fact and begged our pardon.

Codes for Entertainment Media

As most media users expect most media to provide them first with entertainment, it is normal that some of the major grievances people harbor about media concern entertainment. Media stand accused of acting as a drug, exciting or anesthetic—and thus of manipulating the masses to the benefit of a power elite.

Journalism and Entertainment

As mentioned before, the distinction between the two is necessary but is not total. The commercialization of media has led to a corruption of the news by show business. True it is that often the overlap is unavoidable: many news items (spectacular crimes or accidents) partake of entertainment while many movies or TV series are vehicles for knowledge.

Ethics cannot be the same in both sectors. For instance, inaccuracies, invented dialogue, a mix of real and fictional characters and events, the advocacy of a cause: all that is acceptable in a historical drama—and intolerable in a report on today's news. In fact, some of the misdeeds mentioned in codes are due to the confusion between information (useful, important) and entertainment (spicy, thrilling, or pathetic).

There are no codes made by show biz professionals, which is rather surprising as both admen and PR people have some—and also pharmacists and architects. The reason for that? Probably the entertainment trade is too diverse. How could the rules be the same (apart from vague exhortations) for generalist and specialized media: a major TV network and a pay cable channel, a national radio station and an erotic monthly magazine? That said, a number of codes have been devised by show biz employers, which the "artists" have more or less accepted.

Ethics in this field is not entirely different, of course. The same prohibitions are to be found, of racism, for instance, or gratuitous violence. Also, a consensus seems to have developed: similar rules are found in the laws of some nations, in the contractual obligations im-

posed by the French equivalent of the FCC, in the tradition of the
BBC in Britain. For instance, rigging games, morbid sensationalism,
obscenity, incitement to drink alcohol are everywhere considered unacceptable.

However, ethics is also shaped by the dominant values in the surrounding culture. The differences appear when you compare codes or
usage, especially in the reaction of some countries to Western, mainly
U.S., mass culture. Few TV series do not seem pornographic to the
authorities in Saudi Arabia, where local television rarely shows more
than the hands of women.

U.S. Codes

In the U.S., where regulation has always been lighter than in Europe, the codes drafted by entertainment media often deal with issues
that elsewhere are settled by the law: e.g., the maximum amount of
time to be devoted to commercials, the prohibition of advertising for
alcohol or medicinal drugs, or (as far as the late NAB code was
concerned) for fireworks, astrology, and gambling. No false promises,
no commercials presented by self-styled physicians.

What follows is a summary of several U.S. codes, some old and out
of date. First, the famous Hays Code which Hollywood forced upon
itself from the 1930s to the 1960s, under pressure from Catholic and
conservative Protestant groups. It was one of the few codes to be very
precise and to be respected because of a built-in sanction: a movie
found it very hard to be distributed if it did not bear the seal of the
MPAA (Motion Picture Association of America), certifying that the
code had been respected.

The second is the code of good conduct of the NAB, adopted in
1929, often amended and then, in 1962, declared by U.S. courts to be
in violation of the anti-trust laws. It was replaced by a Declaration of
Principles in 1990. Mainly, it inspired the codes which the big networks and many stations gave themselves—and influenced the general behavior of the audiovisual industry. A third source used here is
the internal code of the CBS network.

As an introduction, the Hollywood code stated that "the motion
picture...may be directly responsible for spiritual or moral progress,
for higher types of social life, and for much correct thinking."
Besides, it explained that "correct entertainment raises the whole stan-

dard of a nation." And it stressed the fact that the Seventh Art, contrary to the others, (especially books and the theater) was aimed at all groups in the population, mature and immature, urban and rural, cultured and uneducated.

The Late U.S. Broadcasting Code

The NAB code started from the premise that television should innovate, stimulate creativity, deal with big moral and social issues. It should not only reflect the status quo but "also expose the dynamics of social change."Consequently, it should put on the air a wide gamut of programs, especially cultural and educational. Broadcasters had a special responsibility towards children.

Media entertainment must promote human dignity and fraternity, the value of human life, the respect of rights and different sensibilities. It must support the usages of civilized society. It must avoid all words that generate contempt because of race, religion, nationality, or handicap—except to condemn their use. It must not attack or ridicule religion and Churches. It must not excite the lower instincts. Or foster credulity: e.g., by encouraging belief in astrology or fortune-telling in programs or in commercials.[14] Besides, fiction should not be presented as real events.[15]

Television should find out the needs and desires of its community so as to serve it better. Television professionals must keep in mind that it enters homes and that it has a family audience. It must take into account the needs of children (education, culture, morals) and help the development of their personality. It must uphold respect for marriage and the home, and for the country's institutions. It should not incite to "narcotic addiction" (including cigarette-smoking). It must not present suicide as a solution. Portrayal of sexual acts must be "essential to the plot." The Hays code went further: no costumes, movements, camera angles should offend decency; "nudity is never permitted, in fact or silhouette"; sex perversions should not even be alluded to.[16] On television, any obscene, profane, or indecent material shall not be broad-

---

14. In the past, the ads of quacks contributed to the very bad image of advertising in France. Yet radio and television still accept commercials for astrologers.
15. That clause originates in the panic caused in 1938 by O. Welles' radio adaptation of H.G. Wells' *The War of the Worlds*.
16. Besides, the code forbade to show "miscegenation" (bi-racial couples), to mention venereal diseases, to present "scenes of childbirth."

cast. Also proscribed are unjustified horror, the detailed description of violence, killing, torture, physical agony (including that endured by animals), of any supernatural event likely to horrify. Television "shall not excite interest in" gambling, either in its programs or by commercials. Its games must not be rigged in any way. The law shall not be ridiculed. Greed, selfishness, cruelty shall not be presented in a favorable light. Crime shall not be shown as efficient, justified, or profitable. The techniques of crime shall not be presented in such detail as to be instructional.

Reading those rules is mind-boggling for whoever has watched television in the U.S. or watched U.S. TV programs elsewhere, which nowadays could be any part of the planet. The contrast is striking between the ideals set at the start and what hypercommercialization has gradually produced. It is to be feared that the same is happening to journalism. That gives urgency to the debate over "practical" media ethics, the theme of the present book.

Interpretation and Enforcement of Codes

Interpretation and enforcement are the two problems to be solved after a code is adopted. Its rules are always relatively vague and rarely absolute. As mentioned before, ethics functions at two levels: fundamentals and daily life. The role of media in society needs to be taught, discussed, slowly integrated—and then, every day, reporters and editors have a thousand big or small decisions to make, fast. No code can make provision for every possible case: the professional often has to rely on commonsense or on a "moral sense" born of reflection and discussion. And neither sense, besides, can escape the religious and political tradition of the country, sometimes many centuries old, like tribalism in Africa or feudalism in China.

When in the U.S., newspeople argue whether to publish the name of a rape victim, one simple solution is to ask the person involved. But it is more difficult usually to distinguish between singing the praises of a hometown and concealing its blemishes; between riding a rented bus with a local sports team and accepting a junket to the Bahamas paid for by a maker of sports equipment; between supporting the building of a needed new conference center and currying favor with the publisher who is one of the investors; between respecting the age-old traditions of one's readership and advocating racial segregation.

And so, however useful codes can be, there is a need for something more: the ethical education of journalists. The moral conscience of beginners must be awakened, or reenforced, and they have to be trained in solving everyday problems. Then they need practical experience to interpret the codes, to adapt them to circumstances. The code does help make decisions in emergency situations by tapping the collective wisdom that has emerged from long discussions. But it is quite possible that one professional will reach a decision contrary to that of a colleague who feels just as "responsible" as himself/herself.

Thus when, in a small U.S. town, a little girl came back who had been hideously disfigured in a fire and had undergone long treatment, one newspaper published her photograph and the other did not. One considered that for the child to reintegrate the community, people had to get used to the sight of her. The other preferred not to horrify its readers.

So the journalist, or more often the editor, must call the shots, trying to avoid ideological prejudice, even at the risk of antagonizing part of the audience.

The texts of various codes can be found in the following books or Web sites:

Cooper, Thomas W. (dir.), *Communication Ethics and Global Change* (New York: Longman, 1989).
Geyer, François, *Les codes déontologiques de la presse internationale* (Paris: FIJ et UNESCO, 1975) [mimeographed].
International Press Institute, *Press Councils and Press Codes*, (Zurich: IPI, 4th ed. 1976).

Asian Journalism Network
www.uow.edu.au/crearts/journalism/AJNet.html
Center for Applied Ethics (University of British Columbia)
www.ethics.ubc.ca/resources/media
Illinois Institute of Technology
http://csep.iit.edu/codes/media.html
Institut Français de presse (Université de Paris-2)
www.u-paris2.fr/ifp
Poynter Institute (Florida)
www.poynter.org
University of Tampere (European codes-in English)
www.uta.fi/ethicnet

4

Omissions

Codes proscribe a lot and do not prescribe much, probably because it is easier to agree on faults to avoid than on virtues to practice. But a negative morality is not enough. In this chapter, desirable behaviors are presented which are not often recommended in codes. They originate in the many criticisms which, under various forms, professionals and academics have been making of media for many years. The substance of this chapter has been published in a score of periodicals in over sixteen languages, since 1992:[1] whatever the region of the globe, it seems that these issues are on the agenda.

To Know Oneself and to Master One's Field

A journalist should be conscious of what he/she is and is not: man/woman, white/black, young/old, etc. Many sins committed derive from ignorance of one's nature, talent, and limitations. With a slight exaggeration, ethics might be said to boil down to awareness-raising.

Codes forget to stigmatize the reporter who is content with drawing his/her material from the file provided by a PR service. They do not recommend that he/she do some home-work before going on an assignment, dip into archives (or data banks), and consult experts.[2]

Little is said about preparing for difficult situations like terrorist actions. Terrorism would not exist without the press: it aims at turning the media into amplifiers for the propaganda of a tiny clique. Should

---

1. The latest in a U.S. book: *Impact of Mass Media: Current Issues*, R.E. Hiebert ed. , New York, Longman, 1999.
2. French journalists would be particularly vulnerable in that respect.

media black them out or yield to their demands? Unwise it is to improvise: the research devoted to the topic must be read as well as the many debates.

The need for a journalist to possess wide general knowledge and a special field of expertise: that was one of the major recommendations of the Hutchins Commission. Incompetence takes many forms: the use of undefined terms, the wrong handling of statistics, the simplification of complex issues, presenting hypotheses as proven facts, generalizing from a few cases, drawing unjustified conclusions. Few codes recommend that a newsperson possess firm knowledge in fields like science or law or education or industry—or again in languages for foreign correspondents. Regrets are quite often heard about journalists' lack of competence in economics—but incompetence can affect many diverse fields: it can be political, for instance, when elections take place in some other country, or military and cultural during foreign wars, in Rwanda or Bosnia.

A few years ago, media gave alarming news about a plague epidemic in India, recalling the medieval Black Death that killed over one-third of the population of Europe within three or four years in the fourteenth century—and forgetting to mention that (1) the plague is endemic in India, and (2) it is easy to cure today: there were fewer than 100 deaths.

Last but not least, the codes omit to treat as fundamental the mastery that journalists need to have of their own tongue and the knowledge they must have of their own culture. In France, at least, too many journalists are remarkable by their ignorance of both.

Tradition, Conservatism, Routine

Journalistic usage represents a major obstacle to ethics. Laziness, bureaucratic insensitivity, a failing imagination generate routine: the same areas get covered; the same phenomena are given attention; press releases get published; the same handful of self-appointed experts are consulted. Little consideration is given to excellent but obscure sources like specialized journals and discreet specialists.

Prevalent is "pack journalism": a topic is regarded as worthy of coverage only if it has been touched upon by a major newsservice or the main daily in the country. Then, even if the topic is neither new nor important, everybody rushes in. For a day, a week, or more, it monopolizes media attention—and other far more momentous topics are ignored or given short shrift.

In the 1990s, all French media gave exceptional coverage to AIDS with special issues and programs. There were very few articles or broadcasts, on the contrary, on the major, direct and indirect, causes of death in France, like alcohol and tobacco. If AIDS killed 100,000 people a year, the outcry in the media would be tremendous: such is the number of people killed by the two drugs. What if 500 million human beings were HIV positive? That is the number of people suffering with malaria which, together with sleeping sickness and tuberculosis, destroys more lives in Africa than AIDS.

Single-Track Thinking

When media only carry the views of a small unscrupulous group, then you have a dictatorship, and extreme danger: the Nazis and the Soviets have provided a sad demonstration of it. In a democracy, commercial media preach social conservatism and economic liberalism, while public media usually kowtow to the government. When media champion the status quo too much and grant one ideology a quasi monopoly, a very unhealthy situation develops.

In Japanese "press clubs," which are groups of reporters accredited by political or economic VIPs, journalists get together before a press conference to decide which embarrassing questions not to ask—and after it make sure they all write the same report: a regrettable effect of the Confucian tradition. In a different environment, in the U.S. of the 1950s, media ignored the support given by the U.S. to every fascist regime in the world. They preached the conformist views of the conservative white majority. So the excluded groups rebelled during the following decade, sometimes brutally: Blacks, students, Hispanics, Native Americans, consumers, women, environmentalists, homosexuals, the handicapped, etc.

Fear of Novelty

One role of media is to stimulate change and creativity by introducing new notions, new lifestyles, new products. But in general they are afraid of ideas that are new, nonconformist, or extreme. And their growing commercialization has increased their tendency to preach the bland and intolerant majority culture. They do not censor; they ignore. Unconventional voices are rarely heard, which could provide alternative data and opinions. In the 1960s, it was disturbing to hear U.S. publishers, usually so prone to unsheath the First Amendment, call for the muzzling of the underground press produced by the young radicals. The reign of "political/ social correctness" is much older than some think.

In the journalistic microcosm, the tradition is not challenged enough.[3] The worship of scoops and live reports continues, even though many errors and ethical disasters are due to haste. More generally, there are about a dozen regrettable habits that codes do not seem to consider. Some are linked to the selection of the news, others to the presentation of it. In addition, there are functions media should assume in society which they do not.

Acquisition and Selection

When they set their editorial policy, media managers should be concerned primarily, not about shareholders, advertisers, newssources, but about the public, groups and individuals, everyone who might be affected. This does not appear in the codes in spite of the fact that, outside the media world, firms that have ethical concerns show higher profitability.

Traditionally, media contain human interest stories and political information which, to a large extent, is supplied to them by official agencies. They mention affairs that fall within the consensus or belong with recognized oppositions (center left v. center right, for instance). Media disregard radical fringes, or ridicule them: that was obvious at the rebirth of the feminist movement in the 1960s and 1970s. Media should try and give a full panorama of local, national, international news, which often consists of problems to be solved rather than of acts and accidents.

Omissions

Omission is the worst sin of media. The cause of it can be the very nature of the medium, or a lack of resources, or refusal by the owners to allow some expense. But omission can have other causes. Certain topics are overlooked, partly or totally, because of ancient prejudices and taboos, those of media owners or advertisers (who hardly appreciate consumerism, for instance), those of the young, educated men who fill most newsrooms,[4] or again those of the richer stratum of the

---

3. In each country, the codes should insist on national flaws, e.g. in France, they should stress the need to check facts and to separate news and views.
4. Rape and domestic violence, for instance, got little attention before the proportion of women in newsrooms became important.

public or the majority of the population. Have a look at the following sample of blind spots.

In France, media never investigated the lavish financing of electoral campaigns from the 1960s to the 1980s: yet the money had to come from somewhere. Nor did they investigate corruption in professional sport, especially soccer. Nor the amazing activities of one of the three largest banks, the Crédit Lyonnais, including several billion francs lent to a large press group. Media let the extreme right exploit the irritation felt by the population about growing illegal immigration from Africa. French hospital nurses, truck drivers, school teachers, even policemen have to march down the streets or block the roads for their protests to be heard.

In Japan, at least until recently, tradition prohibited mention of the emperor by the media, Korean immigrant workers, slaughters of Chinese people by Japanese invaders during World War II, the *burakumin* (the untouchable caste), or the *yakusa* mafia. In the U.S., during the four years when the Khmer Rouge controlled Cambodia and killed over a million inhabitants, the ABC network devoted twelve minutes to that country, NBC eighteen, and CBS twenty-nine.

How many media have reported on the genocide of Christians and animists in the Sudan? Were reporters from any country sent to Timor, to report on the massacres there between 1975 and 1995? Is apartheid ever mentioned apart from the now abolished one in South Africa? Where is much attention paid to the way in which women are treated in most Moslem countries (especially to clitoral excision in Africa)?

Information and Entertainment Entwined

One deplorable characteristic of the current debate on media ethics is the omission of entertainment. That is all the more serious as the border between news and entertainment is blurring. Media lack a sense of hierarchy. They should distinguish better between interesting and important news, and focus on that which can affect the life of a social group or of a whole society or of mankind.[5]

On May 6, 1994, the International Herald Tribune devoted almost a quarter of its front page, above the fold to a boxed report on the caning which a young U.S. vandal was about to be given in Singapore.

---

5. In the early 90s, the opposite took place. In the U.S., commercialism pushed quality media towards "tabloïdization," reality shows and docudramas.

On reading this in a U.S. daily, no one would think there were 23,000 murders a year in the U.S.: half as many Americans as were killed during the eight years of the Vietnam war. One murder became the year-long focus of the media in 1994, a banal case, except that the suspect was famous and black while the victim had been gorgeous and promiscuous. U.S. newspaper editors, annually polled by the AP, chose the Simpson case as the number one event of the year. That is almost unbelievable to a European.

Certainly, a medium needs to take its audience into account: while the elite public wants useful data, the popular public likes amusing "factoids." In "middle-brow" media, to be found mainly where there is a local monopoly, the tendency is to mix the two. Now media entertainment is in no way contemptible—but it should not push out or vulgarize true information and become dominant.

Much of what news media are faulted for (appeal to emotions, over-dramatization of news, sometimes the publication of pure fiction) belongs to the entertaining function of media and should be judged by different criteria. Such journalism has been common since the invention of printing; people enjoy it and its influence on them is weak for they are not stupid.

Journalists find it hard to acknowledge that they are, for a part, public entertainers simply because readers/listeners/viewers are "event voyeurs" and look upon a large part of the news as entertainment. And by that I mean not just the sexcapades of some politician or a divorce at the Court of St. James—but also sports results, the spectacular eruption of a distant volcano, a plane crash, or the hold-up of a bank— and even some wars, provided they are not too close.

Pseudo-information

Too many news stories are created by somebody who intends to profit from them: most have the advantage, for media, that they are prepared well in advance and are conditioned for their use. Advertising disguised as news is quite easy to detect in the print media—as is the intense promotion of some books and shows in newscasts or variety programs. Less visible is the press release and/or video clip supplied by PR agents and used by journalists with little or no modification. The same goes for the story written by a journalist after he/she has been treated to a cruise or some other major favor.

Both similar and different is the report on a pseudo-event[6] directed and produced to attract the media, like a presidential press conference or a street demonstration. Or again events fabricated by the media themselves: mini-scandals inflated by self-styled "investigative reporters" or the persecution of celebrities by paparazzi. Such news may very well have some importance but it very much needs to be filtered and labeled. Media users must be told about pseudo-news and where it comes from.

Superficial and Simplistic

Most media do not take into account how complex reality is. They think they have to move fast and amuse, hence they simplify. Therefore, they over-indulge in stereotypes, in the good guys-bad guys dichotomy, in the reduction of phenomena to quaint individuals, of long speeches to sound bites. Thus media give an image of the world and human society that is incomplete, often distorted and that can generate ugly feelings and behaviors.

Media most often present an absurd mosaic of small events. They should be "explaining ...the mechanics of the modern world and show the links between everyday happenings and the deep workings of the forces that shape the fate of society,...point out the premonitory signs of fundamental change in every field."[7] Television especially seems not to be interested in any news item unless there are pictures to go with it: obviously there seldom are easy illustrations for processes and evolutions.

An end should be called to the frantic agitation of journalists always seeking to be the first instead of the best, to such an extent that sometimes they fabricate the event. Such excesses marked the Gulf War. After mindlessly inflating an event (which sometimes never took place[8]), they drop it to jump onto some other one. Few codes demand that a story be followed through to its outcome, that its repercussions be reported.

It is very important that media seek reality under appearances, variously. Codes do not stress the need for journalists to check whatever they quote their sources as declaring, and add a corrective, if it be

---

6.   See Daniel Boorstin, *The Image*, New York, Harper & Row, 1964.
7.   In the code of the Swiss daily *Journal de Genève*, 1971.
8.   like (in 1985) the annual disappearance of thousands of children in the U.S..

warranted. Nor do codes recommend to expose the efforts of sources to manipulate reporters, and to slip their advertising or propaganda into the media: it should be better known that about three-quarters of political and economic information is provided by official sources. Besides, journalists too rarely question a consensus. Between 1945 and 1990, for instance, many incidents indicated that the Soviet Union was not the formidable fortress that it was claimed to be—but media kept mum: could it be because many people had vested interests in the Cold War? Or was it a matter of sheer laziness or stupidity?

There is another way media can unmask reality: it consists in discovering the existence of momentous but invisible phenomena. To do that, one can use the methods of the detective, which is called investigative journalism. In the U.S. at least, it usually forces the police and the courts into action. But journalists should also use social science methods, harness the power of computers to the analysis of archives or surveys, so as to explore under the surface of reality and identify deep movements before they emerge, sometimes as catastrophes.[9] This is bizarrely called "precision journalism" in the U.S.: "test-drilling journalism" might be a better name.

The Half-Empty Glass

Traditionally, good news is no news. What of the end of the war in 1945, the discovery of penicillin, the first man on the moon, or the fall of the Berlin Wall? Media normally stress disagreement, conflict, confrontation, drama, failure[10]: things are going wrong and will be worse. Problems get more attention than solutions; the weird and the criminal more than great achievements. When a piece of news contains a little negative element, that will be the focus of the report. One is led to suspect that newspeople adore automobile pile-ups, slayings, bankruptcies, tornadoes, and political scandals. Cynicism displaces the needed skepticism. All decisionmakers appear as self-centered, incompetent, greedy, and probably dishonest; the mission of the journalist is that of the hero who will expose their wickedness. Corruption should be denounced, certainly, but when the whole of public life is made to seem corrupt, democracy is in danger.

---

9. That was a major aim of the techniques gathered in the 70s by Philip Meyer *The New Precision Journalism*, Bloomington, Indiana UP, 2nd ed. 1991.
10. Very few codes allude to that negativism, e.g. that of the late newspaper *La Suisse* : it recommended that criticism be constructive; and the old U.S. Radio Code required programs that encourage a good adaptation to life.

If a citizen is only presented with the half-empty glass, he/she may well develop a depressing view of a society where actually life is far more pleasant than it used to be fifty or one hundred years ago, at least in the West. And he/she may be discouraged from working at improving his/her fate and that of the community.

Cramped Information

Journalists have an obsession for politics. Nobody can deny that the management of a city, a nation, the planet is important—especially for news media which pride themselves on being a Fourth Estate. But they endow politics with unjustified hegemony. And we may add that media, some of which nowadays function twenty-four-hours-a-day, badger members of government to the point of impeding their activities. "Trying to carry out long-term plans in this environment is like trying to conduct medical research in a hospital emergency room," writes J. Fallows.[11]

First, media should cover economics more (how many French people know that France has the number four GDP in the world?), and social affairs and science. W.R. Hearst rightly remarked that readers were superior in both intelligence and virtue to what many journalists believed. Media must help the public become more learned and civilized, raise its moral level and rationality, preserve past culture and contribute to new cultural forms. Aiming only at the highest common denominator is unethical for its goes contrary to the public interest.

Media should in particular translate and publicize the discoveries and the thoughts of scientists and other experts. Quality dailies, news magazines, and television documentaries do it somewhat but not enough. The media should behave not merely as messengers but also as explorers and initiators. To whet the appetite and enrich the sense of taste is almost as important as to provide food.

Parochialism

Everywhere on the planet, there is a tradition, natural yet regrettable, which is to focus on local and regional news. How amazing it is for a visitor to the U.S. to compare the huge proportion of advertising

---

11. See James Fallows, *Breaking the News*, New York, Pantheon, 1996, page 185.

in dailies (60 percent-70 percent of the total surface) and the tiny proportion of international news (less than 2 percent). It is upsetting also to find that in France most regional dailies consist in a bunch of municipal bulletins with a couple of pages devoted to national and international affairs. Press codes say nothing about that. And yet the general public, whether it is aware of it or not, needs to be informed on the state of the whole earth and the process that has led to that situation.

It is a deplorable fact that there are fewer and fewer correspondents stationed abroad. The special envoys flown into a land when some event there attracts attention are usually ignorant of the country and incapable of understanding it. If foreign bureaus cost too much, then why do not the media in one nation publish articles and air programs made in others? That is what the *Courrier International* (1991) does, a French weekly "reader's digest" of articles translated from all over the world. In Australia, every morning the SBS network airs newscasts from Russia, China, Germany, France, etc. and in the evening regularly broadcasts foreign movies and documentaries. Media could also borrow ideas and techniques from abroad. After all, they are expected to promote better mutual knowledge and understanding, peace and happiness for mankind.

Not Enough About the Media

Another omission in the codes: they do not urge media to report fully on their own business. The relatively recent "Media Sections" indicate new publications and broadcast programs, new executive appointments, firms being bought and sold. Except for major scandals, they give little information on controversies within the media world. With exceptions (usually due to ideological animus or business rivalry), media do not criticize each other: blind eyes are turned on the failings of colleagues. Self-criticism is almost unknown. Extremely rare are the newspapers that publish a "Letter from the Editor" to inform readers about internal affairs. When media do talk about themselves, vaguely, it is to blow their own trumpet.

Do U.S. major television networks have regular programs in which viewers and experts can present their grievances and professionals can reply to them?[12] Was there a special to explain the infamous fabricated Fidel Castro interview (see p. 3) on the French network TF1—

---

12. In the 1990s, this was done by two Australian non-commercial television networks.

and present an apology? The prestigious *Le Monde* is the only daily in France to employ an ombudsman. No newspaper devotes a regular section or page to airing and answering the grievances and suggestions of readers.

Processing and Presentation

Whoever wants to convey an item of information—teacher, story-teller, or journalist— knows that the manner of saying is as important as what is said. Yet rare are the codes that mention the need for printed articles to be attractive (i.e., concise, well-written, well laid-out and illustrated).

Newspapers of Fixed Dimensions

As all the older industries, media believe that they should bring out a product of the same size everyday, with almost the same ingredients, whatever happens on the planet. Consequently, depending on the day, they have either to ignore or neglect important news—or insert some stuffing to fill the allocated amount of space or time. The result is that they give a distorted report on the day's news.

At the end of the twentieth century, a citizen can access all-news radio stations and several all-news TV channels, pioneered by CNN in the 1980s. Also he/she can easily reach out to data banks of texts and images on the Internet. Thanks to computers, it would now be possible, using the material gathered and processed by journalists, to send at any given time "information packages" made according to the stated needs and desires of each subscriber. The packages can vary in size depending on the amount of news and can be distributed at different times, to different places, by very different means.

Incomprehensible News

"The news" often is a heap of events. Now the task of informing is not limited to shoveling out raw data. The journalist should enable the person-in-the-street to understand and evaluate: a structured context must be provided in which to set the news story, and diverse viewpoints must be offered, as well as the considerations of experts. That is indispensable in the case of statistics, opinion polls, speeches by decisionmakers, which need to be compared with other data from the past or from other areas. For D. Boorstin, journalists seem "locked in the present," hence their lack of perspective and appreciation, for instance, of how living conditions have improved over the last century.

Ordinary people are not stupid but many are undereducated and not professionally motivated to keep informed. They find it hard to grasp "the news" because so many words and concepts used by media are unknown to them. So they find the news boring, especially in the printed press. And even if they are interested, most citizens cannot understand an event without being told about the origin of it, its environment, its meaning, and its possible consequences.

There are several possible reasons why journalists do not do it: an old habit of addressing an elite, which has a wide knowledge of the world; lack of time, which is a source of excessive simplification and stereotypes; inadequate training, ignorance, or negligence. Or again, on radio and television, the fear of wearying the audience, which might hurt ratings and shares.

Boring News

Much of the news published is of no use (accidents, crimes of passion, VIP visits). But, unfortunately, useful news often is not very interesting. Wilbur Schramm distinguished between "immediate reward news" and "delayed reward news." If society is to function properly, all its members need to have a good idea of the world around them, near and far. Whether they are naturally inclined or not, it is their duty to be informed. If they are not inclined, then their attention must be caught,[13] by pointing out, for instance, what effect some faraway event can have on their personal lives. That is not an easy task: making important news attractive requires effort, time, and know-how.

Conversely, some news stories that seem merely interesting can be shown to be important for society. A man kills a dozen people on a suburban train: that's a fascinating story with blood, screams, and tears—but what does it say about the environment? About unemployment, destitution, racism, alcoholism, the lack of psychiatric supervision, the unregulated sale of firearms?

---

13. W.R. Hearst thus instructed his publishers "Reward the reporter who can make truth interesting."

The Welfare of Society

Protecting the Weak

One economist[14] noted recently that no famines are allowed to happen in democratic nations, which have a (relatively) free press. Media can do much for citizens and consumers. Unfortunately, they tend to treat people differently depending whether they are powerful or destitute. The elite of newspeople believes it belongs to the Establishment and adopts its preoccupations, yet no code warns against the effect of starification. Freedom of speech and press should be neither the privilege of a caste, nor that of the majority. Radicals, eccentrics, and fringe groups also must be heard. For they are sometimes right. Alas, when the government moves to muzzle protesters, big media have a tendency discreetly to side with the holders of power. In France just as in Japan, they are not the ones to expose abuse. That is usually achieved by small magazines like *Bungei Shunju* or weeklies like the satirical *Canard enchaîné*.

This is not to advocate populist demagoguery. True it is that media too often yield either to majority pressure or to organized lobbies, like farmers in France and the militants of "political correctness" in the U.S. But when the Hutchins Commission recommended that all groups in the population be served, it was thinking of ordinary men and women, whom media do not care too much about, although they are "the people." Codes rarely mention the favorable bias that newspeople show towards the powerful sources of news and media owners. Citizens perceive it as a conspiracy of the holders of power.

"Public Journalism"

The APME[15] Code of ethics (1975, revised in 1994), is one of the very rare codes to make suggestions like the following: "The newspaper should serve as a constructive critic of all segments of society....It should vigorously expose wrongdoing, duplicity or misuse of power,

---

14. Amartya Sen, Master of Trinity College, Cambridge (GB), Nobel Prize for Economics 1998.
15. The association that gathers managing editors of newspapers that are members of the cooperative Associated Press, the largest wireservice in the world.

public or private. Editorially, it should advocate needed reform and innovation in the public interest....The newspaper...should provide a forum for the exchange of comment and criticism, especially when such comment is opposed to its editorial positions."

At the beginning of the 1990s, those notions developed in the U.S. into a controversial new style of journalism, called "public (or civic) journalism." It was invented to counter the media's loss of circulation and credibility. At worst, it belongs with Public Relations, and not that far from prostitution. At best, it usefully stresses that media are, first and foremost, to serve the public, not shareholders, advertisers and political leaders. They should, not stage the news as a show, but inform in order to stimulate the discussion of serious issues, with participation from all kinds of minority groups, even those that make the majority cringe. Thus they can kindle in the citizen a desire to participate in the management of public affairs. Instead of becoming boosters for their town or region, and keeping very prudent, independent media should find out and make known what is not right, suggest solutions to problems, and help citizens to achieve them—even if that proves contrary to ancient usage and vested interests.

The Entertainment Sector

Tradition separates journalism and show business. Nowadays, in fact, the limit between the two is unclear: journalism dresses up more attractively, sometimes outrageously so, while networks are created that specialize in documentaries, history, education—and sports. Sport belongs just as much to the sphere of information as to that of entertainment. Codes almost never mention entertainment but many clauses are applicable to it: objectivity, fairness (no jingoism), no corruption, no incitement to violence, etc.

Similarly, you find that press codes indirectly condemn faults often committed by entertainment media: surreptitious advertising on television or the corruption of DJs; the kind of old-boy networks that keep some artists off the air; and (in France, for instance) excessive profits made by show hosts with their own production companies. But the major criticisms made of them are of a different order and are rarely mentioned in codes. Entertainment media stand accused of promoting stupidity, vulgarity, brutality; of being indifferent to things intellectual and aesthetic; of giving a warped image of the world; of being fundamentally immoral.

Aesthetic Mediocrity

Commercial media make few efforts to innovate, and to promote the more sophisticated forms of creation: literature, (so-called) classical music and the fine arts. Mediocrity sometimes affects even the technique, as in Japanese animated cartoons. To serve their customers well, media should train their taste and refine it. But their huge output makes high quality impossible on a regular basis. A common claim is that their shows are produced on an assembly line by mercenaries and then selected by bureaucrats obsessed with circulation and ratings figures.

Intellectual Vacuum

The commercial media especially are accused of being very reluctant to stimulate the human brain. Television just sells "chewing-gum for the eyes." Even State television does little, with exceptions like the BBC and in Japan the NHK. Everywhere what is sought is the Least Objectionable Program. Users are trained to have a short attention span, to disregard the past, to be always impatient. At worst, media inculcate imbecility by seriously presenting astrology and so-called "paranormal" phenomena. In almost all parts of the globe, and notably in the U.S., the media have ignored their educational function, which probably is their most serious violation of social responsibility.

Moral Mediocrity

Media aim not at training citizens (as schools do) or believers (as the Churches do), but at producing consumers. So they link happiness to consumption, to external signs of success. The values celebrated implicitly are selfishness, greed, and conformity. Everyone is supposed to seek money, fame or some easy cure. All political, economic, and social problems are reduced to the concerns of a few individuals. Some of these people are good guys and the others bad guys; their relationships are power-based conflicts being often solved by fighting, after which order is restored. Thus, media entertainment and advertising, like drugs, create in people both anguish and comfort, dissatisfaction and escape—and eventually frustration and apathy.

Characters in television fiction are stereotyped, with more than a little racism and sexism. Feminine faces and bodies abound but there are few good roles for women. As in the movies, some vast human categories are under-represented: children, old people, intellectuals, blue collars, poor people. In both the programs and the advertising, television gives a simplistic and inaccurate image of the world: it is both embellished (fictional characters often live as if they earn far more than their job can provide) and it is made far more mean and violent than reality. In music videos, men often look like thugs and women like whores: how will that be perceived by immature adolescents? This poses a serious danger for the young in the lower-class urban ghettos who need role models. Also the future as depicted in movie fiction is dark, confined, barbarous (*Terminator, The Eraser, Natural Born Killers*) whereas the world we live in is far less needy and dangerous than it used to be quite recently (1929 Depression, Nazi and Stalinian massacres, Cold war). Thus is conveyed a frustrating, woeful, and false picture of our society.[16]

Violence is omnipresent, in fiction and cartoons as in newscasts— in spite of the fact that family-oriented movies regularly make more money than films of horror and slaughter.[17] In spite of the fact also that innumerable studies have demonstrated the link between media violence and real life violence. At least in the U.S., an explanation is that televised violence excites as much as sex and embarrasses less. U.S. children watch thousands of murders before they leave primary school, yet in the opinion of militant reformers the problem is that they might be exposed to some images of a sexual nature.

Isolationism

For the good of everyone, it is necessary that in every nation media products from other countries be distributed so as to make foreign cultures known and to invigorate its own by hybridization. Not a code even alludes to this. Is it not unethical that in prime time the big U.S. television networks show only 2 percent of foreign products (most of them from Britain)?[18] Actually, the cultural wealth of the U.S. is jeopardized by the protectionism of media that deprive the public of contacts with other cultures. At the same time, U.S. media practice cultural dumping in the rest of the world—in the sense that their television programs, once amortized on the domestic market, are sold

---

16. See M. Medved, *Hollywood vs. America*, New York, HarperCollins, 1993.
17. in 1994, *The Lion King* made far more money than *Pulp Fiction*.
18. See C-J. Bertrand & F. Bordat eds., *Les médias français aux Etats-Unis*, Presses universitaires de Nancy, 1993.

abroad at a small fraction of the price it would cost to make similar programs locally. That causes an erosion of regional creativity. Thus, the culture of both the U.S. and other nations is impoverished. Isolationism is worse in the U.S. but present everywhere. Are there many Indian, Korean, Chilean programs on French television—or even Spanish, Italian, or Swedish programs? How many European programs on Japanese television? Because this causes the public to be badly served, this issue must be considered an ethical issue.

Problems with Advertising

Insofar as media get from advertising a large proportion of their revenues, up to 100 percent, it is bound to influence their behavior. In many countries, the advertising profession has adopted a code of conduct and set up enforcing institutions sometimes stricter than those of media, but media also should be concerned about the contents of ads.

Sometimes, in Western countries, media delegate such ethical concerns to independent institutions, such as the "Bureau de vérification de la publicité" (advertising checking bureau) in France or the Advertising Standards Authority in Britain. Even then, a medium should itself check whether a product for which advertising is forbidden, may be advertised via an ad for another product of the same firm, as mentioned in the NAB television code.

More serious problems occur. When, in 1983, the U.S. television network ABC scheduled *The Day After*, a dark and dramatic picture of the U.S. following a nuclear attack, most advertisers were unwilling to place ads on the program. The situation is even worse when a particular product or service is attacked. Then advertising boycotts generate self-censorship, for instance, that of used car dealers after the local daily publishes advice to would-be customers. More serious still: as far back as the 1930s, the U.S. Federal Trade Commission published reports linking tobacco with fatal ailments. Yet until the 1960s, the media kept silent about the dangers of cigarettes. As late as the 1990s, major U.S. magazines refused the ads of a firm which was launching a campaign for its anti-smoking products.

Fundamentally, Europeans find it insufferable and seemingly immoral (in the sense of "contrary to public service") that over two-thirds of the surface of dailies be occupied by ads, and that television programs be interrupted every nine or ten minutes by loud clusters of commercials—as in the U.S.

5

A Selection of Codes

It would be of little use to reprint here documents that are well known in the U.S., like the excellent codes of the SPJ-SDX or those of the APME. All the codes presented here are non-U.S. One is international. Of the next three—national—the first was adopted by newspaper publishers in Britain, the second by a union of journalists in Russia, and the third by the press council of India. Hence they are very different from each other. The last code in the selection consists in a specific set of rules for reporters of small events (largely crimes and accidents) in the French provincial press. Many other codes deserve to be cited, like that of the Japanese NSK or that of South Africa. The problem is that the reading of codes tends to be painfully monotonous, since most of them say just about the same.

An International Declaration
of the Rights and Obligations of Journalists

Approved in 1971 by representatives of the journalists' unions of six countries of the European Community, in Munich (Germany).

Preamble

The right to information, to freedom of expression and criticism is one of the fundamental rights of man.

All rights and duties of a journalist originate from this right of the public to be informed on events and opinions.

The journalist's responsibility towards the public excels any other responsibility, particularly towards employers and public authorities.

The mission of information necessarily includes restrictions which journalists spontaneously impose on themselves. This is the object of the declaration of duties formulated below.

A journalist, however, can respect these duties while exercising his profession only if conditions of independence and professional dignity effectively exist. This is the object of the following declaration of rights.

Declaration of Duties

The essential obligations of a journalist engaged in gathering, editing and commenting news are:

1. To respect truth, whatever be the consequences to himself, because of the right of the public to know the truth;

2. To defend freedom of information, comment and criticism;

3. To report only on facts of which he knows the origin; not to suppress essential information nor alter texts and documents;

4. Not to use unfair methods to obtain news, photographs or documents;

5. To restrict himself to the respect of privacy;

6. To rectify any published information which is found to be inaccurate;

7. To observe professional secrecy and not to divulge the source of information obtained in confidence;

8. To regard as grave professional offences the following: plagiarism, calumny, slander, libel and unfounded accusations, the acceptance of bribe in any form in consideration of either publication or suppression of news;

9. Never to confuse the profession of a journalist with that of advertisements salesman or a propagandist and to refuse any direct or indirect orders from advertisers;

10. To resist every pressure and to accept editorial orders only from the responsible persons of the editorial staff.

Every journalist worthy of that name deems it his duty faithfully to observe the principles stated above. Within the general law of each country, the journalist recognizes, in professional matters, the jurisdiction of his colleagues only; he excludes every kind of interference by governments or others.

Declaration of Rights[1]

1. Journalists claim free access to all information sources, and the right to freely inquire on all events conditioning public life. Therefore, secret of public or private affairs may be opposed only to journalists in exceptional cases and for clearly expressed motives.
2. The journalist has the right to refuse subordination to anything contrary to the general policy of the information organ to which he collaborates such as it has been laid down by writing and incorporated in his contract of employment, as well as any subordination not clearly implicated by this general policy;
3. A journalist cannot be compelled to perform a professional act or to express an opinion contrary to his convictions or his conscience;
4. The editorial staff has obligatorily to be informed on all important decisions which may influence the life of the enterprise. It should at least be consulted before a definitive decision on all matters related to the composition of the editorial staff e.g. recruitment, dismissals, mutations and promotion of journalists is taken.
5. Taking in account his functions and responsibilities, the journalist is entitled not only to the advantages resulting from collective agreements but also to an individual contract of employment, ensuring the material and moral security of his work as well as a wage system corresponding to his social condition and guaranteeing his economic independence.

**The Code of Practice
of the British Press Complaints Commission**[2]
(1994, revised 1997)

All members of the press have a duty to maintain the highest professional and ethical standards. This code sets the benchmarks for those standards. It both protects the rights of the individual and upholds the public's right to know.

---

1. Most of which in fact are the duties of media towards the journalists working for them.
2. The PCC (1991), and its predecessor the Press Council (1953), were set up to try and curb the excesses of the popular national press (*Sun, Mirror, Mail* etc.), which accounts for many clauses in the code.

The code is the cornerstone of the system of self-regulation to which the industry has made a binding commitment. Editors and publishers must ensure that the code is observed rigorously not only by their staff but also by anyone who contributes to their publications.

It is essential to the workings of an agreed code that it be honoured not only to the letter but in the full spirit. The code should not be interpreted so narrowly as to compromise its commitment to respect the rights of the individual, nor so broadly that it prevents publication in the public interest.

It is the responsibility of editors to co-operate with the PCC as swiftly as possible in the resolution of complaints.

Any publication which is criticised by the PCC under one of the following clauses must print the adjudication which follows in full and with due prominence.

1. Accuracy

i. Newspapers and periodicals should take care not to publish inaccurate, misleading or distorted material including pictures.
ii. Whenever it is recognised that a significant inaccuracy, misleading statement or distorted report has been published, it should be corrected promptly and with due prominence.
iii. An apology must be published whenever appropriate.
iv. Newspapers, whilst free to be partisan, must distinguish clearly between comment, conjecture and fact.
v. A newspaper or periodical must report fairly and accurately the outcome of an action for defamation to which it has been a party.

2. Opportunity to reply

A fair opportunity for reply to inaccuracies must be given to individuals or organisations when reasonably called for.

3. Privacy

i. Everyone is entitled to respect for his or her private and family life, home, health and correspondence. A publication will be expected to justify intrusions into any individual's private life without consent.

ii. The use of long lens photography to take pictures of people in private places without their consent is unacceptable.

Note—Private places are public or private property where there is a reasonable expectation of privacy.

4. Harassment

i. Journalists and photographers must neither obtain nor seek to obtain information or pictures through intimidation, harassment or persistent pursuit.

ii. They must not photograph individuals in private places (as defined by the note to clause 3) without their consent; must not persist in telephoning, questioning, pursuing or photographing individuals after having been asked to desist; must not remain on their property after having been asked to leave and must not follow them.

iii. Editors must ensure that those working for them comply with these requirements and must not publish material from other sources which does not meet these requirements.

5. Intrusion into Grief or Shock

In cases involving personal grief or shock, enquiries should be carried out and approaches made with sympathy and discretion. Publication must be handled sensitively at such times but this should not be interpreted as restricting the right to report judicial proceedings.

6. Children

i. Young people should be free to complete their time at school without unnecessary intrusion.

ii. Journalists must not interview or photograph a child under the age of 16 on subjects involving the welfare of the child or any other child in the absence of or without the consent of a parent or other adult who is responsible for the children.

iii. Pupils must not be approached or photographed while at school without the permission of the school authorities.

iv. There must be no payment to minors for material involving the welfare of children nor payments to parents or guardians for material about their children or wards unless it is demonstrably in the child's interest.

v. Where material about the private life of a child is published, there must be justification for publication other than the fame, notoriety or position of his or her parents or guardian.

7. Children in Sex Cases

1. The press must not, even where the law does not prohibit it, identify children under the age of 16 who are involved in cases concerning sexual offences, whether as victims or as witnesses.
2. In any press report of a case involving a sexual offence against a child:

> i. The child must not be identified.
> ii. The adult may be identified.
> iii. The word "incest" must not be used where a child victim might be identified.
> iv. Care must be taken that nothing in the report implies the relationship between the accused and the child.

8. Listening Devices

Journalists must not obtain or publish material obtained by using clandestine listening devices or by intercepting private telephone conversations.

9. Hospitals

i. Journalists or photographers making enquiries at hospitals or similar institutions should identify themselves to a responsible executive and obtain permission before entering non-public areas.
ii. The restrictions on intruding into privacy are particularly relevant to enquiries about individuals in hospitals or similar institutions.

10. Innocent Relatives and Friends

The press must avoid identifying relatives or friends of persons convicted or accused of crime without their consent.

11. Misrepresentation

Journalists must not generally obtain or seek to obtain information or pictures through misrepresentation or subterfuge.
i. Documents or photographs should be removed only with the consent of the owner.
ii.) Subterfuge can be justified only in the public interest and only when material cannot be obtained by any other means.

12. Victims of Sexual Assault

The press must not identify victims of sexual assault or publish material likely to contribute to such identification unless there is adequate justification and, by law, they are free to do so.

13. Discrimination

i. The press must avoid prejudicial or pejorative reference to a person's race, colour, religion, sex or sexual orientation or to any physical or mental illness or disability.
ii. It must avoid publishing details of a person's race, colour, religion, sexual orientation, physical or mental illness or disability unless these are directly relevant to the story.

14. Financial Journalism

i. Even where the law does not prohibit it, journalists must not use for their own profit financial information they receive in advance of its general publication, nor should they pass such information to others.
ii. They must not write about shares or securities in whose performance they know that they or their close families have a significant financial interest without disclosing the interest to the editor or financial editor.
iii. They must not buy or sell, either directly or through nominees or agents, shares or securities about which they have written recently or about which they intend to write in the near future.

15. Confidential Sources

Journalists have a moral obligation to protect confidential sources of information.

16. Payment for Articles

i. Payment or offers of payment for stories or information must not be made directly or through agents to witnesses or potential witnesses in current criminal proceedings except where the material concerned ought to be published in the public interest and there is an overriding need to make or promise to make a payment for this to be done. Journalists must take every possible step to ensure that no financial dealings have influence on the evidence that those witnesses may give.

(An editor authorising such a payment must be prepared to demonstrate that there is a legitimate public interest at stake involving matters that the public has a right to know. The payment or, where accepted, the offer of payment to any witness who is actually cited to give evidence should be disclosed to the prosecution and the defence and the witness should be advised of this).

ii. Payment or offers of payment for stories, pictures or information, must not be made directly or through agents to convicted or confessed criminals or to their associates—who may include family, friends and colleagues—except where the material concerned ought to be published in the public interest and payment is necessary for this to be done.

The Code of Professional Conduct
of the Russian Journalist

Adopted by the Congress of Russian Journalists on 23 June 1994 in Moscow.

1. A journalist is obliged always to act on the basis of the principles of the professional ethics set in this Code, the approval, acceptance and observance of which is an absolute condition for his membership in the Russian Federation of Journalists.

2. A journalist observes the law of his country, but when the fulfillment of his professional duty is concerned he recognizes the jurisdiction of his colleagues only, and rejects any attempted pressure and interference from the government or anyone else.

3. A journalist only disseminates, and comments upon, information whose reliability he has ascertained and whose source is well known to him. He will strive as hard as he can to avoid any damage, to whoever it may be, caused by the incompleteness or inaccuracy of a story; he will avoid the deliberate concealment of socially important information and the dissemination of all information known to be false.

A journalist must absolutely separate the facts he is reporting and any opinions and assumptions, but that does not mean he is obliged to be neutral in his professional activities.

When fulfilling his professional duties, a journalist will not resort to illegal and unworthy methods of acquiring information. A journalist recognizes and respects the right of individuals and institutions not to give information and not to answer the questions presented to them, excluding the cases in which the presentation of information is required by law.

A journalist considers the malevolent distortion of facts, slander, the obtaining of payment for dissemination of false information or the hiding of truthful information, under any circumstances, as a serious professional crime; generally speaking, a journalist should not take, either directly or indirectly, any kind of compensation or reward from third persons for the publication of any kind of material or opinion.

When convinced that he has published false or distorted material, a journalist must correct his mistake using the same print and/or audio-visual media which were utilized to publish the original material. If need be, he must present his apologies.

A journalist's name and reputation stand as a guarantee of the reliability of all the messages and for the fairness of all the judgements that are disseminated with his signature, pseudonym or anonymously yet with his knowledge and approval. No one has the right to forbid him to withdraw his signature from a news story or comment, which has been even only partly distorted against his will.

4. A journalist respects professional secrecy in relation to the source of any information that is acquired in a confidential way. No one can force him to reveal this source. The right to anonymity may be broken only in exceptional cases when there is suspicion that the source consciously has distorted the truth, and also when the reference to the name of the source is the only way to avoid serious and inevitable damage to the people.

A journalist is obliged to respect the request of the persons interviewed by him to keep their statements as background and not publish them with attribution.

5. A journalist understands fully the danger of restraints, persecutions and violence, which his activities may provoke.

In fulfilling his professional duties, he must oppose extremism and any restriction of civil rights on the basis of sex, race, language, religion, political views, as well as social or national origin.

A journalist respects the honor and dignity of the people who become the objects of his professional attention. He refrains from any derogatory allusions or comments in relation to race, nationality, skin color, religion, social origin or sex as well as to a physical handicap or disease. He refrains from publishing that kind of information except when it is directly relevant to the content of the published article. A journalist must absolutely avoid offensive speech which may harm the moral and physical health of people.

A journalist sustains the principle that any person is innocent so long the opposite has not been demonstrated in court. In his reports he avoids mentioning the names of the relatives and friends of persons found guilty or charged with committing a crime - excluding circumstances when that is needed for the objective presentation of the case. He also avoids mentioning the names of the victims of the crime and publishing the kind of material which can lead to the identification of the victim. These norms should be observed with particular strictness when media reports could harm the interests of minors.

Only the defense of the interest of society may justify journalistic investigations which imply intrusion into the private lives of people. These restrictions on invasion of privacy must be strictly observed rigorously in the case of persons placed in medical or related institutions.

6. A journalist considers his professional status incompatible with holding positions in organs of the executive, legislative or judicial power. The same applies to the governing bodies of political parties or other organizations of a political nature. A journalist recognizes that his professional activities cease when he takes a weapon into his hands.

7. A journalist considers it unworthy to use his reputation, his authority, his professional rights and capabilities in order to disseminate

information of an advertising or commercial nature, especially if this kind of material is not clearly evident from the very form of the material. The combination of a journalistic and an advertising activity is ethically unthinkable.

A journalist should not use in his personal interest, or that of his kin, any confidential information which he may possess because of his profession.

8. A journalist respects and defends the professional rights of his colleagues and observes the rules of fair competition. A journalist keeps away from situations in which he might cause harm to the personal or professional interests of his colleagues, by agreeing to fulfill their duties in conditions which are well known to be socially, materially or morally less favored.

A journalist respects copyright and demands that others respect it, concerning any kind of creative work. Plagiarism is inadmissible. When he utilizes in any form the work of a colleague, a journalist cites the name of the author.

9. A journalist refuses an assignment if to fulfill it he will have to violate one of above-mentioned principles.

10. A journalist uses and asserts his right to use all guarantees provided by the civil and penal laws as a defense in the court or by other means against violence or the threat of violence, insult, moral damage or defamation.

Third World Code from India

NORMS OF JOURNALISTIC CONDUCT[3]
(1992, revised 1996)

Principles and Ethics

The fundamental objective of journalism is to serve the people with news, views, comments and information on matters of public interest in a fair, accurate unbiased, sober and decent manner. Towards this end, the Press is expected to conduct itself in keeping with certain

---

3.   It should be remembered that Indian English can be quite different from U.S. English.

norms of professionalism universally recognised. The norms enunciated below and other specific guidelines appended thereafter when applied with due discernment and adaptation to the varying circumstance of each case, will help the journalist to self-regulate his or her conduct.

Accuracy and Fairness

1. The Press shall eschew publication of inaccurate, baseless, graceless, misleading or distorted material. All sides of the core issue or subject should be reported. Unjustified rumours and surmises should not be set forth as facts.

Pre-publication Verification

2. On receipt of a report or article of public interest and benefit containing imputations or comments against a citizen, the editor should check with due care and attention its factual accuracy apart from other authentic sources with the person or the organisation concerned to elicit his/her or its version comments or reaction and publish the same with due amendments in the report where necessary. In the event of lack or absence of response, a footnote to that effect should be appended to the report.

Caution against Defamatory Writings

3. Newspaper should not publish anything which is manifestly defamatory or libellous against any individual or organisation unless after due care and checking, they have sufficient reason to believe that it is true and its publication will be for public good.
4. Truth is no defence for publishing derogatory, scurrilous and defamatory material against a private citizen where no public interest is involved.
5. No personal remarks which may be considered or construed to be derogatory in nature against a dead person should be published except in rare cases of public interest, as the dead person cannot possibly contradict or deny those remarks.
6. The Press shall not rely on objectionable pad behaviour of a citizen for basing the scathing comments with reference to fresh action of that person. If public good requires such reference, the Press should make

pre-publication inquiries from the authorities concerned about the follow up action, if any, in regard to those adverse action.

7. The Press has a duty, discretion and right to serve the public interest by drawing reader's attention to citizens of doubtful antecedents and of questionable character but as responsible journalists they should observe due restraint and caution in hazarding their own opinion or conclusion in branding these persons as 'cheats' or 'killers' etc. The cardinal principle being that the guilt of a person should be established by proof of facts alleged and not by proof of the bad character of the accused. In its zest to expose the Press should not exceed the limits of ethical caution and fair comments.

8. Where the impugned publications are manifestly injurious to the reputation of the complainant, the onus shall be on the respondent to show that they were true or to establish that they constituted for comment made in good faith and for public good.

Parameters of the right of the Press to comment on the acts and conduct of public officials

9. So far as the government local authority and other organs/ institutions exercising governmental power are concerned, they cannot maintain a suit for damages for acts and conduct relevant to the discharge of their official duties unless the official establishes that the publication was made with reckless disregard for truth. However judiciary, which is protected by the power to punish for contempt of court and the parliament and Legislatures, protected as their privileges are by Articles 105 and 194 respectively, of the Constitution of India represent exception to this rule.

10. Publication of news or comments/information on public officials conducting investigations should not have a tendency to help the commission of offences or to impede the prevention or detection of offences or prosecution of the guilty. The investigating agency is also under a corresponding obligation not to leak out or disclose such information or indulge in disinformation.

11. The Official Secrets Act 1923 or any similar enactment or provision having the force of law equally bind the press or media though there is no law empowering the state or its officials to prohibit, or to impose a prior restraint upon the press/media.

12. Cartoons and caricatures in depicting good humour are to be placed in a special category of news that enjoy more liberal attitude.

Right to Privacy

13. The Press shall not intrude upon or invade the privacy of an individual unless outweighed by genuine overriding public interest, not being a prurient or morbid curiosity. So, however, that once a matter becomes a matter of public record, the right to privacy no longer subsists and it becomes a legitimate subject for comment by Press and media among others.

> Explanation: Things concerning a person's home, family, religion, health, sexuality, personal life and private affairs are covered by the concept of PRIVACY excepting where any of these impinges upon the public or public interest.

14. Caution against identification: While reporting crime involving rape, abduction or kidnap of women/females or sexual assault on children, or raising doubts and questions touching the chastity, personal character and privacy of women, the names, photographs of the victims or other particulars leading to their identity shall not be published.

15. Minor children and infants who are the offspring of sexual abuse or 'forcible marriage' or illicit sexual union shall not be identified or photographed.

Recording interviews and phone conversation

16. The Press shall not tape-record anyone's conversation without that person's knowledge or consent except where the recording is necessary to protect the journalist in a legal action, or for other compelling good reason.

17. The press shall, prior to publication, delete offensive epithets used by an interviewer in conversation with the Press person.

18. Intrusion through photography into moments of personal grief shall be avoided. However, photographs of victims of accidents or natural calamity may be in larger public interest.

Conjecture, comment, and fact

19. Newspapers should not pass on or elevate conjecture, speculation or comment as a statement of fact. All these categories should be distinctly stated.

Newspapers to eschew suggestive guilt

20. Newspapers should eschew suggestive guilt by association. They should not name or identify the family or relatives or associates of a person convicted or accused of a crime, when they are totally innocent and a reference to them is not relevant to the matter reported.

21. It is contrary to the norms of journalism for a paper to identify itself with and project the case of any one party in the case of any controversy/dispute.

Corrections

22. When any factual error or mistake is detected or confirmed, the newspaper should publish the correction promptly with due prominence and with apology or expression of regrets in a case of serious lapse.

Right of Reply

23. The newspaper should promptly and with due prominence publish either in full or with due editing, free of cost, at the instance of the person affected or feeling aggrieved or concerned by the impugned publication, a contradiction/reply/clarification or rejoinder sent to the editor in the form of a letter or note. If the editor doubts the truth or factual accuracy of the contradiction/reply/clarification or rejoinder, he shall be at liberty to add separately at the end a brief editorial comment doubting its veracity, but only when this doubt is reasonably founded on unimpeachable documentary or other evidential material in his/her possession. This is a concession which has to be availed of sparingly with due discretion and caution in appropriate cases.

24. However, where the reply/contradiction or rejoinder is being published in compliance with the discretion of the Press Council, it is permissible to append a brief editorial note to that effect.

25. Right of rejoinder cannot be claimed through the medium of Press Conference, as publication of a news of a conference is within the discretionary powers of an editor.

26. Freedom of the Press involves the readers' right to know all sides of an issue of public interest. An editor therefore shall not refuse to publish the reply or rejoinder merely on the ground that in his opinion

the story published in the newspaper was true. That is an issue to be left to the judgement of the readers. It also does not behove an editor to show contempt towards a reader.

Letters to editor

27. An editor who decides to open his columns for letters on a controversial subject, is not obliged to publish all the letters received in regard to that subject. He is entitled to select and publish only some of them either in entirety or the gist thereof. However in exercising this discretion he must make an honest endeavour to ensure that what is published is not one-sided but represents a fair balance between the views for and against with respect to the principal issue in controversy.
28. In the event of rejoinder upon rejoinder being sent by two parties on a controversial subject, the editor has the discretion to decide at which stage to close the continuing column.

Obscenity and vulgarity to be eschewed

29. Newspapers/journalists shall not publish anything which is obscene, vulgar or offensive to public good taste.
30. Newspapers shall not display advertisements which are vulgar or which, through depiction of a woman in nude or lewd posture, provoke lecherous attention of males as if she herself was a commercial commodity for sale.
31. Whether a picture is obscene or not, is to be judged in relation to three tests; namely

    i. Is it vulgar and indecent?
    ii. Is it a piece of mere pornography
    iii. Is its publication meant merely to make money by titillating
    the sex feelings of adolescents and among whom it is intended to
    circulate? In other words, does it constitute an unwholesome
    exploitation for commercial gain.

Other relevant considerations are whether the picture is relevant to the subject matter of the magazine. That is to say, whether its publication serves any preponderating social or public purpose in relation to art, painting, medicine research or reform of sex.

Violence not to be glorified

32. Newspapers/journalists shall avoid presenting acts of violence armed robberies and terrorise activities in a manner that glorifies the perpetrators' acts, declarations or death, in the eye's of the public.

Glorification/encouragement of social evils to be eschewed

33. Newspapers shall not allow their columns to be misused for writings which have a tendency to encourage or glorify social evils like Sati Pratha[4] or ostentatious celebrations.

Covering communal disputes/clashes

34. News, views or comments relating to communal or religious disputes/clashes shall be published after proper verification of facts and presented with due caution and restraint in a manner which is conducive to the creation of an atmosphere congenial to communal harmony, amity and peace. Sensational, provocative and alarming headlines are to be avoided. Acts of communal violence or vandalism shall be reported in a manner as may not undermine the people's confidence in the law and order machinery of the State. Giving community-wise figures of the victims of communal riot, or writing about the incident in a style which is likely to inflame passions between the tension, or accentuate the strained relations between the communities/religious groups concerned, or which has a potential to exacerbate the trouble, shall be avoided.

Headings not to be sensational/provocative and must justify the matter printed under them

35. In general and particularly in the context of communal disputes or clashes;
    a. provocative and sensational headlines are to be avoided;
    b. Headings must reflect and justify the matter printed under them;
    c. Headings containing allegations made in statements should either identify the source making it or at least carry quotation marks.

---

4.   The sacrifice of the wife at the funeral of the husband.

Caste, religion or community references

36. In general, the caste identification of a person or a particular class should be avoided, particularly when in the context it conveys a sense or attributes a conduct or practice derogatory to that caste.
37. Newspapers are advised against the use of word "Scheduled Caste" or "Harijan"[5] which has been objected to by some persons.
38. An accused or a victim shall not be described by his caste or community when the same does not have anything to do with the offence or the crime and plays no part either in the identification of any accused or proceeding, if there be any.
39. Newspaper should not publish any fictional literature distorting and portraying the religious characters in an adverse light transgression of the norms of literary taste and offending the religious susceptibilities of large section of society who hold those characters in high esteem, invested with attributes of the virtuous and lofty.
40. Commercial exploitation of the name of prophets, seers or deities is repugnant to journalistic ethics and good taste.

Reporting on natural calamities

41. Facts and data relating to spread of epidemics or natural calamities shall be checked up thoroughly from authentic sources and then published with due restraint in a manner bereft of sensationalism, exaggeration, surmises, unverified facts.

Paramount national interest

42. Newspapers shall, as matter of self-regulation, exercise due restraint and caution in presenting any news, comment or information which is likely to jeopardise, endanger or harm the paramount interests of the State and society, or the rights of individuals with respect to which reasonable restrictions may be imposed by law on the right to freedom of speech and expression under clause (2) of Article 19 of the Constitution of India.
43. Publication of wrong/incorrect map is a very serious offence, whatever the reason, as it adversely affects the territorial integrity of the country and warrants prompt and prominent retraction with regrets.

---

5. "People of god," the term used by Gandhi for the untouchable the lowest social castes.

Newspapers may expose misuse of diplomatic immunity

44. The media shall make every possible effort to build bridges of co-operation, friendly relations and better understanding between India and foreign States. At the same time, it is the duty of a newspaper to expose any misuse or undue advantage of the diplomatic immunities.

Investigative journalism, its norms and parameters

45. Investigative reporting has three basic elements.
   a. It has to be the work of the reporter, not of others he is reporting;
   b. The subject should be of public importance for the reader to know;
   c. An attempt is being made to hide the truth from the people.

i. The first norm follows as a necessary corollary from (a) that the investigative reporter should, as a rule, base his story on facts investigated, detected and verified by himself—and not on hearsay or on derivative evidence collected by a third party, not checked up from direct, authentic sources by the reporter himself.

ii. There being a conflict between the factors which require openness and those which necessitate secrecy, the investigative journalist should strike and maintain in his report a proper balance between openness on the one hand and secrecy on the other, placing the public good above everything.

iii. The investigative journalist should resist the temptation of quickies or quick gains conjured up from half-baked, incomplete, doubtful facts, not fully checked up and verified from authentic sources by the reporter himself.

iv. Imaginary facts, or ferreting out or conjecturing the non-existent should be scrupulously avoided. Facts, facts and yet more facts are vital and they should be checked and cross-checked whenever possible until the moment the paper goes to press.

v. The newspaper must adopt strict standards of fairness and accuracy of facts. Findings should be presented in an objective manner, without exaggerating or distorting, that would stand up in a court of law, if necessary.

vi. The reporter must not approach the matter or the issue under investigation in a manner as though he were the prosecutor or counsel for the prosecution. The reporter's approach should be fair, accurate and balanced. All facts properly checked up, both for and against the core issues should be distinctly and separately stated, free from any one-sided inferences or unfair comments. The tone and tenor of the report and its language should be sober, decent and dignified, and not needlessly offensive, barbed, derisive or castigatory, particularly while commenting on the version of the person whose alleged activity or misconduct is being investigated. Nor should the investigative reporter conduct the proceedings and pronounce his verdict of guilt or innocence against the person whose alleged criminal acts and conduct were investigated, in a manner as if he were a court trying the accused.

vii. In all proceedings including the investigation, presentation and publication of the report, the investigative journalist/ newspaper should be guided by the paramount principle of criminal jurisprudence, that a person is innocent unless the offence alleged against him is proved beyond doubt by independent, reliable evidence.

viii. The private life, even of a public figure, is his own. Exposition or invasion of his personal privacy or private life is not permissible unless there is clear evidence that the wrong doings in question have a reasonable nexus with the misuse of his public Position or power and has an adverse impact on public interest.

ix. Though the legal provisions of Criminal procedure do not in terms, apply to investigating proceedings by a journalist, the fundamental principles underlying them can be adopted as a guide on grounds of equity, ethics and good conscience.

Confidence to be respected

46. If information is received from a confidential source, the confidence should be respected. The journalist cannot be compelled by the Press Council to disclose such source; but it shall not be regarded as a breach of journalistic ethics if the source is voluntarily disclosed in proceedings before the Council by the journalist who considers it necessary to repel effectively a charge against him/ her. This rule requiring a newspaper not to publish matters disclosed to it in confidence, is not applicable where:

    a. consent of the source is subsequently obtained; or

    b. the editor clarified by way of an appropriate foot-note that since the publication of certain matters were in the public interest, the information in question was being published although it had been made "off the record."

Caution in criticising judicial acts

47. Excepting where the court sits 'in-camera' or directs otherwise, it is open to a newspaper to report pending judicial proceedings, in a fair, accurate and reasonable manner. But it shall not publish anything:
• which, in its direct and immediate effect, creates a substantial risk of obstructing, impeding or prejudicing seriously the due administration of justice; or
• is in the nature of a running commentary or debate or records the paper's own findings, conjectures, reflection or comments on issues sub judice and which may amount to arrogation to the newspaper the functions of the court; or
• regarding the personal character of the accused standing trial on a charge of committing a crime.
Newspaper shall not as a matter of caution, publish or comment on evidence collected as a result of investigative journalism, when, after the accused is arrested and charged, the court becomes seized of the case: Nor should they reveal, comment upon or evaluate a confession allegedly made by the accused.
48. While newspapers may, in the public interest, make reasonable criticism of a judicial act or the judgement of a court for public good; they shall not cast scurrilous aspersions on, or impute improper motives or personal bias to the judge. Nor shall they scandalise the court or the judiciary as a whole or make personal allegations of lack of ability or integrity against a judge.
49. Newspaper shall as a matter of caution avoid unfair and unwarranted criticism which, by innuendo, attributes to judge extraneous consideration for performing an act in due course of his/her judicial functions, even if such criticism does not strictly amount to criminal Contempt of Court.

Newspapers to avoid crass commercialism

50. While newspapers are entitled to ensure, improve or strengthen their financial viability by all legitimate means, the Press shall not engage in crass commercialism or unseemly cut-throat commercial competition with their rivals in a manner repugnant to high professional standards and good taste.
51. Predatory price wars/ trade competition among newspapers, laced with tones disparaging the products of each other initiated and carried

on in print assume the colour of unfair trade, repugnant to journalistic ethics. The question as to when it assumes such an unethical character is one of the fact depending on the circumstances of each case.

Plagiarism

52. Using or passing off the writings or ideas of another as one's own, without crediting the source, is an offence against the ethics of journalism.

Unauthorised lifting of news

53. The practice of lifting news from other newspapers and publishing them subsequently as their own, ill-comports with the high standards of journalism. To remove its unethicality, the 'lifting' newspaper must duly acknowledge the source of the report. The position of features articles is different from 'news' : Feature articles shall not be lifted without permission/proper acknowledgement.
54. The press shall not reproduce in any form offending portions or excerpts from a proscribed book.

Non-return of unsolicited material

55. A paper is not bound to return unsolicited material sent for consideration of publication. However when the same is accompanied by stamped envelope the paper should make all efforts to return it.

Advertisements

56. Commercial advertisements are information as much as social, economic or political information. What is more, advertisements shape attitude and ways of life at least as much as other kinds of information and comment. Journalistic propriety demands that advertisements must be clearly distinguishable from editorial matters carried in the newspaper.
57. Newspaper shall not publish anything which has a tendency to malign wholesale or hurt the religious sentiments of any community or section of society.
58. Advertisements which offend the provisions of the Drugs and Magical Remedies (Objectionable Advertisement) Act, 1954 should be rejected.

59. Newspapers should not publish an advertisement containing, anything which is unlawful or illegal, or is contrary to good taste or to journalistic ethics or proprieties.

60. Newspapers while publishing advertisements, shall specify the amount received by them. The rationale behind this is that advertisements should be charged at rates usually chargeable by a newspaper since payment of more than the normal rates would amount to a subsidy to the paper.

61. Publication of dummy advertisements that have neither been paid for nor authorised by the advertisers, constitute breach of journalistic ethics.

62. Deliberate failure to publish an advertisement in all the copies of a newspaper offends against the standards of journalistic ethics and constitutes gross professional misconduct.

63. There should be no lack of vigilance or a communication gap between the advertisement department and the editorial department of a newspaper in the matter of considering the propriety or otherwise of an advertisement received for publication.

64. The editors should insist on their right to have the final say in the acceptance or rejection of advertisements, specially those which border on or cross the line between "decency and obscenity."

65. An editor shall be responsible for all matters, including advertisements published in the newspaper. If responsibility is disclaimed, this shall be explicitly stated beforehand.

Specialized Sector
Ouest-France Code
for reporting crimes and accidents (Extracts[6])

I. The "human interest story" (HIS) is in a double sense the keystone of the news,
—from the reader's viewpoint, it's a priority center of attention [...].
—from the reporter's viewpoint, the HIS calls into play the fundamental professional rules, at the highest degree (checking of facts, contradictory sources, investigative rigor, reflection, sensitivity, respect for the human being [...] to be applied on an unstable, complex, unpredictable, aberrant and hazardous terrain).

---

6. In French "Code du fait-diversier", a "fait-divers" being a "human interest story" normally reported by quality papers as "news in brief."

Whether small or big, every HIS involves our legal and ethical responsibility. It requires a minimal knowledge of the law and legal procedures, the capacity to find the right tone, somewhere in-between the coldness of a clinical examination and over emotionalism.

The HIS reaches in the depths of people. It triggers sensibilities, probes consciences and disturbs the existing balance in communities.

The reporter assigned to HIS [...], in the story he/she tells of the event, of the investigation and possible sequels, must constantly seek to embody the values of justice, freedom, respect of individuals and of their rights, which are the foundation of the newspaper *Ouest-France*. [...]

II. Basic Principles

● The HIS, checked, precise and understandable, must be reported with the permanent preoccupation of the possible repercussions of the publication (for the people directly involved, for the family of the victims, for the family of the guilty...)

● The facts must be put in context, in their human dimensions, with no concession to voyeurism.

● Facts, small and big, must be followed up systematically. The reporter will not hesitate to return to facts that remain mysterious, unsolved. He/she will be humble enough to give the end of the story even if it contradicts what he/she had written in his/her earlier reports.

● The facts should be accompanied with testimonies, interviews that help to understand—also with information likely to help the reader not be the victim of a similar HIS.

● Reporters should be extremely careful about attributing causes, linking cause and effect, defining the responsibility of each of the people involved. What seems obvious might not be true and sources may be trying to manipulate the press [...]

V. HIS and the Operation of Newsrooms

In county-level newsrooms, a HIS specialist is needed. There should be no daily rotation. At worst, the assignment to HIS should be on a weekly basis so as to allow some follow-through. Processing HIS requires knowledge, specific investigating methods, networks of informers. [...]

Beware: what seems obvious may not be true. Police sources are often overconfident. Beware of confessions made during the investigation. [...]

Words are not neutral. Let us be specially vigilant with the vocabulary we use [...] Let us ban words that hurt and for which there are easy substitutes, let's proscribe phrases that steer public opinion and the jury towards presuming guilt (e.g., "the character is well-known of the police," [...] "the murderer refuses to admit the facts."). [...]

Lower Courts. Coverage of them provides a mine of information on the evolution of delinquency and society. It should not be treated as a pillory! Most cases can be treated as social events, without names being revealed. [...]

What is interesting is not to "nick Mr. So-and-so": it is the fact and the punishment dealt out ("what do I face if the same misadventure happens to me?") [...]

VI. Little Guide for the HIS Reporter

Accidents. The causes, even as mentioned in the police report, should be presented with caution. The publication of them can influence the possible court action.

The report of an accident should be supplemented in case there is a problem with the roads or with traffic management.[...]

Suicides. The rule is not to mention them [...].

Minor Crimes. [...] The reporter, of course, keeps his freedom of appreciation to evaluate the gravity of the facts and the context. Experience proves that dialogue with his team and the hierarchy can best guarantee of coherence and fairness.

[...] Do not implicate by name people who are not directly involved in the case. Do not implicate a profession, an ethnic or religious group with such headlines as "Murder by a Psychiatrist," "The Thief was a Fireman," "An Algerian Burglar"...

Beware of the racist connotations of certain phrases: do not write "A Moslem Frenchman"; would you say "A Catholic Frenchman"? Do not use derogatory terms.... If the alleged criminal is a foreigner (check the fact) specify what nationality he is and whether he is a resident in France.

Rape. Do not publish the identity of the victim or any element that could help identification (unless the victim insist it be published, in writing, according to article 39 of the law of 23 December 1980).

Incest. The law prescribes total anonymity. Identification is possible if a court action has been initiated by an adult victim who wants publicity around the case.

Indecent exposure. In all cases, anonymity is required if the identity of the accused may lead to identification of under-age victims. Extreme caution is necessary during the investigation. [...].

Infanticides. Describe the circumstances, the context, the social environment, with tact and intelligence, avoiding to cause shame and humiliation to anyone. That requires sympathy and good judgment. Anonymity should be total until the trial, with few exceptions. [...]

Part 3

Quality Control

6

The M*A*S
Media Accountability Systems

Media ethics faces one crucial problem: finding means to enforce its rules that are acceptable, that is to say non-governmental. How can a human being be incited to behave well? Three kinds of pressure can be brought to bear. Human perversity makes it necessary that, for the good of other members of society, he/she be submitted to an external physical pressure. Human nobility makes him/her sensitive to principles and values—hence to an internal moral pressure. Human ambivalence makes it possible that an external moral pressure be enough, the kind of influence that rules of professional ethics exert through the reprobation of peers or contempt of the public when a violation is committed.

In the press, for centuries, only the first two of those three disciplines were used. A virtuous journalist obeyed his conscience; the unscrupulous hack had to face the constabulary and the courts. At the turn of the twenty-first century, it is becoming indispensable to use the third discipline if we are to enjoy a free and democratic press. Now that media have turned into big business, the individual conscience is inadequate. As regards the law, the magistrates and the police, they are not much trusted for they have too often been used to muzzle the press.

Hence the concept of M*A*S: any non-State means of making media responsible towards the public. Because the concept is global, it is rather vague. It includes individuals and groups, regular meetings, written documents, small media or again a long process or a particular approach. Normally, M*A*S act only by moral pressure. But their

107

action can be reinforced by the authority of media executives or pre-existing legal obligations.

In France and the U.S., and the rest of the world, "talking" about ethics became fashionable in the 1990s, but seldom does anyone consider "doing" anything. Very regrettably, journalists who write books about ethics brush aside scornfully the suggestion that any means be used to enforce the rules. For many years everywhere, most newspeople have ignored or dismissed all M*A*S by claiming that they are threats to press freedom, to human rights, to democracy. With untypical restraint, a well-known French columnist stated that "any ethical supervision would be totalitarian!" Others get furious at the mere thought even of a code of conduct. So the present chapter will be anathema to many media professionals, be they European or U.S.

The Participants

Whoever undertakes to check the quality of media services to the public, must first make sure that the media have elected as their primary purpose to serve the public. Then the needs and desires of the public must be ascertained. Lastly, one must verify that they are satisfied. The three parties involved (owners, professionals, and users) can do the checking in various ways, separately or together. A participation of legislators is not advisable but it does exists in some countries, like India, and, if kept to a minimum, causes few problems. Normally, the State should not participate, except by delivering the threats that media often need to start the process of self-regulation.

Media Owners

They might be expected to set up their own quality control systems, but few industries have ever, in the absence of external pressure, even given themselves a code of ethics, not to speak of enforcing it. In a monopoly situation, prosperity puts conscience to sleep. In a competitive situation, a few unscrupulous individuals, who refuse any kind of ethics, will force all others to follow suit.

Editors and News Directors

Obviously, the simplest, least expensive, most efficient means of enforcing a code is to ask newsroom executives to do it. That is easy

when the code is included in the hiring contract: the retribution (repri-
mand, demotion, suspension, firing) can then be quick, even immediate.

But if management acts alone, ill effects are to be expected. Newsroom executives stand in an ambiguous position: they are journalists
and also, to a large degree, agents of the owner. To the extent that
management's first concern is profit, it can hardly be in charge of
ethics (= good public service). It will be tempted to ignore some slip
because it benefits its interests. Actually, it might itself have incited
its employee to commit the sin. In case of a public outcry, it will be
tempted to use the reporter as a scapegoat—not to speak of using the
code to get rid of staff that do not toe the line.

Newspeople

They, of course, are the most involved. They can benefit most from
an improvement in the quality of media—being those who are usually
held responsible for the mediocrity of them. The earlier version of the
RTNDA code[1] ended with: "Broadcast journalists shall actively cen-
sure and seek to prevent violations of these standards and shall actively encourage their observance by all journalists." In fact, unions
and associations, though they do sometimes set up disciplinary committees, are always very reluctant to punish.

The code of the Federation of Arab Journalists (1972) requires that
professionals denounce their colleagues when they misbehave. That
"is not done" in Western democracies—but is peer solidarity acceptable in case of very serious violations of ethics, like systematic faking,
blackmail, or moonlighting for an intelligence service?

In theory, the voluntary cooperation of journalists and publishers to
impose on the press a socially responsible behavior would be an efficient and simple solution, but the public might not trust it much.
Experience[2] has shown that any guild-like professional body sets a
priority on its own interests and neglects self-criticism.

Media users

They are too often forgotten in the debate about ethics. They themselves, alas, believe they are powerless against media, unless they sue.

---

1. U.S. Radio Television News Directors Association.
2. That, for instance, of the original British "General Council of the Press" (1953-1963)
    which had no public members.

But they are reluctant to go to court—and would probably never go if there was some other way to get heard. Could they act alone? Maybe one day consumer defense associations will finally worry about the media as they have long done with yogurt, microwave ovens and banking services. Militant citizens could get together and, with the help of experts in social communication, analyze media contents critically, even collect complaints from the public and process them. But if they did, the professionals can be expected, as usual, to reject all grievances. And it would be too easy for them to deprive critics of their sole weapon: publicity for their activities.

So the cooperation of professionals and public seems to be most often indispensable. Professionals know best how to improve the media and are motivated to do so but are too few and too vulnerable to confront economic and political forces alone. They need the support of the masses of media users with their great voting and purchasing power.

A Brief History

All the "media accountability systems" (M*A*S) that are going to be discussed here exist. They have been tested and found satisfactory. Many actually were conceived and realized in the U.S., probably because the media are more commercialized there than anywhere else and because people fear State regulation more than anywhere else.

Interest in the M*A*S was weak until the 1960s. Then a threshold of exasperation was passed. Several symbolical events signaled the evolution. In 1967, local press councils were set up and the first ombudsman was appointed by a daily newspaper; from 1968, there was a flowering of highly critical "journalism reviews"; then, in 1971, a regional press council was organized in Minnesota, and in 1973 a national news council. Those innovations seemed to indicate two conversions: some owners accepted that their employees had "a voice in the product"; and some journalists accepted that the public also was entitled to a say.

At the turn of the 1970s, much attention was paid to "press councils" when the UNESCO, the International Press Institute, the Council of Europe and, in the U.S., the 20th Century Fund and the Mellett Foundation, funded symposiums and experiments. There was a flood of reports, articles, books on the topic. The press council is potentially the most efficient M*A*S because it gathers the three media protagonists, but it is not the only M*A*S by far: there are about forty of them. Some certainly exist that have escaped attention—and new ones could be devised.

The Basic Means

Training

That is the long-term solution to most problems of quality: the education of citizens in the use of media and a college education for professionals. Old-style on-the-job training was practical but myopic—and it has now become dangerously insufficient. The university can give journalists (a) general culture and (b) specialized knowledge in a field, and (c) an ethical awareness.[3] The future journalist can thus be made competent and responsible, hence respected and more autonomous.

Evaluation

The oldest method to improve the media, the easiest, the most common, is criticism, positive and negative. It normally comes from politicians, of course, from business leaders, minority spokesmen, consumerists, environmentalists, and intellectuals. But it should also come from two other groups: first, the media professionals themselves, whose credibility is strongest, and secondly, from communication scholars who can use scientific methods in the evaluation.

Monitoring

It is needed nowadays because media products are extremely numerous and many of them are short-lived. Also because so often media sins are sins of omission, difficult to spot. Only independent, academic experts can afford an extended observation of media, the analysis of their contents over long periods and research into their long-term effects.

Feedback

How can media dream of serving society well without listening to the grievances of the various categories of media users and of mem-

---

3. But two thirds of U.S. journalism professors rarely or never teach a stand-alone ethics course. *Editor & Publisher*, 12 Sept. 1998 - p.14.

bers of every social institution? Studies have shown the frequent gap between the tastes of users and the perception that media executives have of those tastes. Decisionmakers need to be better informed than by simply scrutinizing sales and ratings curves. One method consists in hiring journalists who are different (women, ethnic minorities). And this can help solve another problem, the access to media of minorities that wish to publish their news and opinions.

In practice, a given M*A*S can combine several of those approaches: a monthly like the *American Journalism Review*[4] criticizes, monitors, lets the voice of users be heard and informs journalists. What follows now is a (non-exhaustive) catalogue of M*A*S, distributed according to their basic nature.

Written and Broadcast Documents

Correction Box

That tool may seem negligible but it is not. For one thing, it has the rare advantage of costing nothing. Mainly, it counters a traditional flaw of the press: its reluctance to admit its errors. With this M*A*S, provided they make it visible, newspeople advertise that they no longer claim to be infallible. They thus improve their credibility (contrary to what was long believed in the profession) and the trust of the public.

If necessary, the brief mea culpa can turn into an extended and tough self-examination like that by the *Washington Post* ombudsman after staff member Janet Cooke faked a story and had to give back her Pulitzer prize.

"Letters to the Editor"

One main function of media is to provide a "forum." In a democracy, all groups in the population need to express themselves. And not just via institutions like unions or ethnic associations. Hence the value of this M*A*S. In the U.S., it developed greatly in the 1970s to the extent, in some dailies, of taking up more than a whole page next to editorials. It is one of the best-read sections. Some radio and television stations also devote some time to the mail they receive and to "guest

---

4. Now published by the Journalism School at the University of Maryland to which, in 1987, a businessman gave a million dollars to carry on the good work with the JR.

columns". And more and more media now get immediate feedback from their readers on-line. Some publish the e-mail addresses of their staff.

Paid-for Opinion Pages

Some firms (like Mobil Oil) or ideological groups in the U.S. buy pages in periodicals to denounce what they perceive as sins of the media. A former assistant of President Reagan once bought two pages in the *Washington Post* to refute the version that daily had given of his brother's death. This is very rare in other parts of the world.

Accuracy and Fairness Questionnaire

They are supposed to be mailed from time to time to people who have been mentioned in the newspaper[5]—or they are published for all readers to fill out. Have they noticed any factual mistake or signs of bias? In the second version, this M*A*S costs little, so it is amazing that it is so little used.

Internal Memo

The various editors in a newsroom should behave as pedagogues: they must from time to time remind everyone of the principles of journalism and of the in-house rules, even when there exists a great, but unwritten, tradition founded many years ago by some mythic newsman, like Hubert Beuve-Méry at the French daily *Le Monde*.

Code of Ethics

A code endorsed by media professionals after discussion is a M*A*S to the extent that it is known. Then its mere existence exerts a moral pressure. In the U.S., where a majority of newspapers possess a code of conduct, some publish it from time to time which brings the public into the game.

In 1994, the Federation of Russian Journalists adopted a code: whoever signed it obtained a professional ID card from the union (signed by the president of the International Federation of Journalists) which brought him/her various perquisites, like access to information and insurance.

---

5. like the *Seattle Times* or again the daily *Globo* in Rio de Janeiro (Brazil).

Media Page/Program

Not only should such pages contain news about media but also criticism. Nowadays, they can be found in quality dailies and newsmagazines. An equivalent can exist in radio and television, like *Mediawatch*, a weekly thrashing of media on the ABC network in Australia or like *Inside Story* (1981-85) produced in the U.S. by the non-commercial network PBS.

Journalism Review

Mainly since the late 1960s, JRs, monthlies or quarterlies, local or national, have been devoted to the criticism of the media of a town or a country, to the spotting of distortions and omissions and to the publication of news that the regular media have ignored (see infra p. 124).

Few JRs were ever broadcast but in the mid-1990s some appeared on the Web. Cyber-JRs attacked the media in a traditional way but could also offer journalists a board where to denounce the inner workings of their media.

The Public Statement

The opinions given by a VIP on media can have great impact, either because of the position of the speaker, as in the case of Vice President Spiro Agnew's 1969 diatribes against liberal media; or because of the striking wording of their pronouncements, like FCC chairman Newton Minnow's description of U.S. television as "a vast wasteland" (1961); or both, like Lenin's sinister definition of the functions of the press. A picture can do much also like that of reelected President Truman holding up a copy of the *Chicago Tribune* with the headline "Dewey Wins."

The Critical Report or Book

Reports drawn up by committees of experts on the initiative of consumer associations (like MTT in France[6]) or State institutions (like the Senate in the U.S.), sometimes on the occasion of some crisis,

---

6. A French association of television viewers, founded in 1990, which is supported by two traditionally incompatible NGOs, one an association of school teachers, the other an association of (Catholic) families.

reveal what media have done wrong, or not at all—and they suggest improvements. That is just what some books also do that are written or edited by professionals like Ken Auletta, or by outside observers, like Leo Bogart, many of them academics, like Larry Sabat, while some that can wear two caps like Philip Meyer.[7]

The Movie or Television Program

Some films show the world of newspapers, radio stations, and television in a realistic (*Absence of Malice*, 1981) or satirical (*Network*, 1976) light—as do some televised series, realistic (*Lou Grant*, 1977-82) or sarcastic (*WKRP in Cincinnati*, 1979; *Murphy Brown* 1988-98) manner.

Alternative Media

Much information that otherwise might not reach the general public is carried by party bulletins, alternative newspapers, political talk shows, private non-commercial FM stations, or rented channels on local cable systems. Similarly, in authoritarian regimes, the *samizdat* (clandestine publications) carry information and implicitly stigmatize the regular media—as do underground or foreign-based radio stations and satellite television and audio and video cassettes.

Public Broadcasting

Is that a M*A*S? Yes, insofar as it devotes itself to public service and, by its very existence, represents a denunciation of profit-oriented broadcasting: no advertising break every ten minutes, no low-grade demagogic entertainment, no filtering of the news by the multinational firms that provide the commercial medium with most of its revenues. Public broadcasting generates true competition, whose effects can be excellent: evidence can be found in Britain and Japan.

---

7. K. Auletta, *Three Blind Mice: How the TV Networks Lost Their Way*, New York, Vintage, 1992; L. Bogart, *Commercial Culture, The Media System and the Public Interest*, New York, Oxford UP, 1995; L. Sabbat, *Feeding Frenzy: How Attack Journalism Transformed American Politics*, New York , Free Press, 1991; P. Meyer, Ethical Journalism, New York, Longman, 1987.

Individuals and Groups

The Regulatory Agency

To the extent such a State commission does not take orders from the government and considers its primary purpose is to protect the public, it can (almost) be looked upon as a M*A*S. In their warnings and reports, the CSA in France, and the FCC in the U.S. expose the faults of broadcasting, its deceptions and sensationalism, etc. The commission also receives complaints, a little like press councils. However, their mission is to enforce principles formulated by a Parliament. Thus they stand on the margin of the realm of ethics.

In Britain, the Broadcasting Standards Commission was set up on the recommendation of the 1996 Broadcasting Act. Endowed with quasi-judicial powers, it is meant to process complaints by listeners and viewers of both public and commercial broadcasting. It can demand the recordings of programs, explanations from producers and, if need be, the publication of its conclusions.

The Media Reporter

Media always tend to keep quiet about their own business. Yet, now that they have become one of the nervous systems in the social body, the public needs to be informed about them. Some journalists must specialize in that field so as to cover its news well and investigate uncompromisingly. One of the most renowned such experts is David Shaw, of the *Los Angeles Times*, who, in 1991, was awarded the first Pulitzer Prize for media criticism. His long reports (e.g., on sports journalism or the press-police relationship) stand half-way between JR articles and university studies.

The In-house Critic

In the U.S., a few newspapers have hired an "in-house critic." The Japanese have had *shinshashitsu* since 1922: those "commissions for the evaluation of contents" are to be found in every major daily as also in news agencies and at the HQ of the NSK, the association of newspaper publishers. Every day a team of journalists scrutinizes the newspaper and reports on any violation of the code. In some cases, it also deals with the "letters to the editor," and fields complaints. There, in the press sector, you find the "quality control" that has given Japanese products their worldwide reputation.

Ethical Coaching

The in-house critics are sometimes expected to contribute to the ethical training of the staff. That can also be achieved by "ethics committees" made up of journalists who ponder ethical issues, give their views on cases as they happen, set up workshops and, if need be, draft a code. There are also "editorial councils" made up of both editors and reporters. They are supposed to brief the newly hired. A newspaper can also, from time to time, obtain the services of an ethics coach from the outside, as the *Philadelphia Inquirer* once did.

The Ombudsman

Most often, the mediator's function is assumed by an experienced journalist, employed by a newspaper, like the *Washington Post* or *El Pais* (in Spain), by a broadcast station, or again by some huge institution like the Canadian Broadcasting Corporation. His/her role is to listen to angry readers/viewers, to investigate their complaints and, when the case is serious, to publish his/her conclusions in a weekly column. He/she needs to be respected by his/her peers and have nothing to expect or fear from the hierarchy. The "reader's advocate," another name used, opens a door to the public, proves that the medium is ready to consider criticisms. The advantage of this M*A*S: ease of access and quick reaction. The problem: if the ombudsman is to be efficient, he/she must be perceived neither as a defender of the medium nor as a mouthpiece of the customers, a tough balancing act.

The first "ombudsman" was appointed by the *Louisville Courier-Journal* in 1967.[8] Actually, the very first probably dates back to 1913, when Joseph Pulitzer started his Bureau of Accuracy and Fair Play to field complaints at his New York *World*.

In 1989, R. Chandler, a highly respected U.S. publisher suggested a similar M*A*S: an arbitration panel set up by a newspaper when

---

8. The Swedish press ombudsman, appointed in 1969, is attached to the Press Council, not to a media outlet.

threatened with a libel suit, which would consist of external experts and whose findings on the case would be published.

The Liaison Committee

In the U.S., the first M*A*S of this kind were "free press/fair trial committees" bringing together journalists and lawyers to help each group understand the other's requirements and to ward off the risk of an official muzzle, like that forced upon the British media under the pretext of insuring fair trials. In France, in the 1970s, unions of journalists, magistrates and police set up such a committee. A liaison should be sought by newspeople with any group they might clash with at the expense of the public interest, like some group of recent immigrants, and also protest groups.

The Local Press Council

That term covers the regular meetings (often quarterly) of representative citizens of a community with leaders of the media, on the initiative of an outside institution, like a school of journalism or an association of consumers, or, more often, that of a publisher.[9] Media users are offered an opportunity to express their grievances and wishes—and also to learn how media operate, and so become more tolerant.

For a number of years, the *Journal-Star* of Peoria (Illinois) asked a housewife in each of its twenty-one distribution zones to question inhabitants of her neighborhood at random about what they liked and disliked in the newspaper. On the occasion of a lunch at the daily, once a month, the members of this original press council reported their findings and a summary was published the next day over one or two pages.

Quite similar is the "jury of consumers," a dozen readers or viewers chosen as being representative of the market, which a medium questions once or on a regular basis about what they think of its performance. They are paid for each session, the discussion being stimulated by an experienced chairperson.

The National, or Regional, Press Council

The best-known M*A*S can be found in all Nordic, Germanic, and Anglo-Saxon democracies—as well as in countries as diverse as India,

---

9. A newspaper can go further (like the *Press-Herald* of Portland, Oregon) and appoint members of the public to its board.

Chile, Ghana, Israel, and Estonia. Normally now, a press council brings together representatives of press owners, of journalists, and of the public to examine complaints against the media—and to defend the freedom of the press. Its only weapon is the publication of its judgments (see infra p. 127)

The Media-related NGO

Some "quality control" operations, occasional or regular, are conducted by groups with media connections, like unions (such as the SNJ, Syndicat national des journalistes, in France), or guild-like associations (such as SPJ-SDX in the U.S.), or NGOs (like the Project for Excellence in Journalism). Or again by independent foundations, like those created in the U.S. by press tycoons to promote education, research, and other means of improvement, like the Freedom Forum. In the 1960s and 1970s, such diverse groups played a great part in the launching or survival of M*A*S. Alas, no such foundation has ever been set up in France by media groups like Havas, Hachette, or conglomerates with large media holdings like Vivendi.

The Media Observatory

A study center that observes the behavior of media and reports publicly on their failings. It can be scientific. Very often, especially in the U.S., it is militant, either on the left and, more commonly, on the right. Specialized or not, they try and prove that media distort the news and pollute the public mind. A remarkable monitoring job has been done since 1976 by Project Censored, initiated and managed by Carl Jensen at Sonoma State University (California): a panel of media critics has drawn up an annual list of the "Ten Best Censored Stories," i.e., important events which media have underplayed, often for obvious reasons.

The Association of Militant Citizens

They can be highly intolerant and/or single-issue movements which, for instance, publish lists of TV programs they dislike and the names of advertisers that sponsor them, a tactic that sometimes works. At best, they are associations of media users which try and influence media with sensitization meetings, letter-writing campaigns, opinion surveys, systematic evaluations, appeals to law-makers, complaints addressed to regulatory agencies, suits, and also boycotts.

In the U.S., Action for Children's Television (1968) has won remarkable victories on behalf of children. In France in 1996, MTT, under the aegis of UNESCO, gathered in Paris representatives of viewers' associations from Europe and Canada. In a very different region, Niger, in the recent past, an association united many radio-clubs which organized collective listening and sent in criticism and suggestions.

The Disciplinary Committee

It can be set up within an Order of Journalists (like the Italian Ordine dei Giornalisti) or a guild-like associations (such as ASNE in the U.S.) or again, most often in Europe, within a union of journalists. Experience proves that it is always discreet and rarely severe: it tends to find excuses for its members.

The "Société de rédacteurs"[10]

Seldom does the staff wholly own the medium it works for (as was the case of most newspapers in Slovenia following the post-communist privatization). But, in theory at least, it is easier for an association of newspeople to own shares in the firm for which they work, not as an investment but in order to have a say in the determination of the editorial policy. The first to attract attention was the one at the daily *Le Monde* in 1951. Such associations exist at the French public broadcasting institutions, but are only active in times of crisis. That M*A*S is rare.

The "Société d'usagers"[11]

Even rarer perhaps is the association of citizens that acquires shares of a media firm and then demands to have a word to say in the management of it—like the "société des lecteurs" of *Le Monde* in Paris. One very remarkable case is that of cable systems in Manitoba (Canada). Media users there won their fight against huge companies that looked forward to million-dollar profits. They obtained that the board of management of every system be elected every year in each community.

---

10. Literally, a "company of journalists" somewhat as in a "company of actors."
11. Literally, a company of (media) users. Infra, "lecteurs" means "readers."

Processes

Higher Education

A journalist trained on the job, or in a strictly vocational school, may find it difficult not to be a "mercenary scribbler," ever treated as a general assignment reporter, deferential to the hierarchy and the local VIPs—too much concerned by his/her personal interest and too little by ethics.

The risk was clear in the 1990s in Black Africa and Eastern Europe. The new generation of reporters that suddenly replaced the media *nomenklatura* of a dictatorial regime, was often incompetent both in journalism and ethics.

Nowadays, more than three-quarters of the younger French and U.S. journalists have been to college. And the mutual antagonism between media people and academics has waned. The university being more independent than other institutions from both government and business, it can provide a base for many M*A*S—in addition to its experts and its ideas.

What universities lack is money. Media companies everywhere should financially encourage the higher education of their professionals, as many do in the U.S.: grants to schools, mid-career fellowships, subsidies for research.

Continuous Education

Every journalist needs to improve his/her competence in a special field and also sometimes to move away from the newsroom for an extended period to do a little thinking about the job and the responsibilities attached to it. That can be done in a one-week seminar, or during a semester on campus, or even a whole sabbatical year, like the Journalism Fellowships, now funded thanks to a grant by press tycoon John Knight, which make it possible every year for about twenty mid-career journalists to study at Stanford University. Or like the Nieman Fellowships at Harvard.

One-day workshops (within the newspaper,[12] or outside) are organized by professional associations, journalism schools, or NGOs. Being practical, using case study or role playing, they re-enforce the

---

12. In the U.S., two thirds of newspapers have some workshops (*Newspaper Research Journal*, Winter 1992).

awareness journalists have of their duties and provide them with guidelines in their relationship with sources, employers, and the public.

Media in the Schools

The proportion of their lives that people devote to media is large enough to justify that they learn about them and know how to use them to their advantage. All children need to be taught critically about the structures of media, their contents, their effects, which implies more than the existing Newspapers in Education programs, sponsored by the press. Students need to be trained to consume media intelligently—and even to make them, by working for high school newspapers or radio stations.

Consulting with Users

In the U.S. at the beginning of the 1990s, a fashion in the newspaper press was "reader call-in nights": some evenings, the various editors would take calls from readers. A variant of that consists, during the lunch break, for journalists to converse with some guest about his/her activities in the community.

More commonly, meetings between professionals and citizens can take place in some press club. Or the newspaper can organize "town meetings" where reporters question local people about their concerns, and what they expect from the local media. Then they can help them mobilize and try to solve their problems (see "civic journalism," p. 74). More and more commonly, the exchanges take place on media Web sites.

The Opinion Survey

Radio, having become commercial early, felt the need to prove the size and nature of its listenership to its advertisers—as television did later. Up to the sixties, the printed press was content with getting its circulations checked. Competition has now become fiercer and all media wish to know what their "demographics" are and what are the views/needs/desires of each layer of their potential audience, so as better to seduce it and sell it to particular advertisers.

The motivation is commercial but the effect is that of a M*A*S. Following the great pioneer Lazarsfeld, commentators often contrast "administrative" research (done for the media) and "critical" research (done for the public). Actually, there is much overlap.

The Ethical Audit

Any news medium needs to have its ethical level checked from time to time. How accurate and unbiased are its stories? Are its internal rules known, understood, followed by the staff? What does its audience think of its services? Are its contacts with the public sufficient, efficient? What could be done to better the situation? A simple check can raise consciousness and modify behaviors.

Non-profit Research

That is done by universities, or by independent institutes, like the Observatoire européen de l'audiovisuel, in Strasbourg (France) or the Media Studies Center in New York. The U.S. has many think tanks funded by foundations. All employ experts equipped to conduct in-depth studies, especially empirical studies that produce accurate figures. Media criticism can no longer be solely based on random examples and anecdotes. The argument over media ethics is too often a rhetorical fight, an exchange of vague accusations and impressionistic retorts. There is a need for concrete data drawn from the analysis of contents and non-contents, from audience surveys and from historical comparisons.

Those studies are particularly necessary (1) to perceive the omissions and prolonged distortions committed by the media.[13] And (2) to evaluate the effects of media operations in a society, especially on a long-term basis. Hence to suggest a better way of doing things.

That ends the catalogue of M*A*S. They can also be listed according to their origin: some function within the media industry, some outside of it, and others require a cooperation of media and public.

---

13. E.g. D.J. Krajicek, *Scooped! How the Media Have Missed the Real Story on Crime While Chasing 'Crime Waves', Sleaze and Celebrities,* New York, Columbia UP, 1998.

Internal M*A*S

Correction box	Code of ethics
Media reporter	Ethical audit
In-house critic	Ethics coach
Disciplinary committee	Ombudsman
Media page/program	Opinion survey
Internal memo	Company of journalists

External M*A*S

Journalism review	Higher education
Alternative media	Media at school
Critical book/report	Consumer group
Public statements	Association of militant citizens
Media-related NGO or Foundation	Company of users
Media observatory	Public broadcasting
Non-profit research	Regulatory agency

Cooperative M*A*S

Letters to the editor	Liaison committee
Public access	Local press council
Paid-for opinion page	National/regional press council
Accuracy and fairness questionnaire	Continuous education
Consulting with users	Movie or TV series

Two Special M*A*S

Journalism Reviews[14]

The most famous JR was created by a Department of Journalism (*Columbia JR,* 1961) - but the pioneer, G. Seldes' *In Fact* (1940-50) and the reviews of the golden age (1968-75), like the *Chicago JR,* were launched by exasperated working journalists. None of the latter have survived , for lack of funds, of readership and of devoted staff. Both the *American JR* (ex-*Washington* JR) and the *St. Louis JR* have been handed over to universities. In the 1990s, non-campus JRs are partisan, left-wing (*Extra!* 1986) and mainly right-wing (*Media Monitor*).

What JRs showed, at the turn of the 1970s, was that some reporters at least were not submissive wage-earners: they could protest publicly. That new attitude has spread. Union periodicals had always been aggressive, but those of professional associations became so. Even scholarly journals have since been more inclined to expose the failings of media.

One popular initiative of the [*MORE*] (1971-78), the only JR to aim at making a profit, was to create the Liebling prize. Criticism should also be positive and be materialized in various rewards: compliments, promotion, salary raise, local or national awards. Whoever might doubt their efficiency should remember those Hollywood moguls who hung in their offices the framed congratulatory letters they had received from movie-goers.

The newspeople who founded those reviews in the U.S. between 1968 and 1975, received little encouragement from media-linked institutions that could have been expected to support the movement. Press Clubs showed little interest. The creators of JR often were militants in the only union (TNG[15]), but the union was content with (vainly) exhorting its local chapters to help JRs financially. On the other hand, the creators usually worked for unionized newspapers and were thus protected. The Association of Educators in Journalism and Mass Communication (AEJMC) was uninterested. As for schools and departments of journalism, out of sixty accredited, twelve encouraged the

---

14. See C-J. Bertrand, "A Look at Journalism Reviews", *FoI Center Report* (University of Missouri) N° 0019, September 1978, one of the very few studies of JRs.
15. The Newspaper Guild since merged with the International Typographical Union and in the mid-90s with Communication Workers of America.

JRs. Only one of the national foundations helped. Business circles were more generous than the media microcosm.

The major obstacle, however, was the small size of the journalistic community and the low degree of interest shown by the public. In cities of 500,000 inhabitants or more, most JRs sold only 500 to 2,000 copies. The revenues of JRs were bound to be small. Most were produced by a little group of reporters who had more idealism, more courage, more free time, or simply less to lose than their colleagues. They did not know much about the management of a periodical. The indifference that greeted their crusade eroded their morale; the hostility it bred was hard to endure. Gradually, their fire went out. Usually there was nobody with the zeal or the talent to take over the JR.

The second major obstacle was the arrogance or paranoia of publishers, editors, and many reporters. Their allergy to criticism was such that they refused to give JRs the slightest publicity—and so the reviews remained unknown to the general public. Some newspaper executives screamed High Treason and undertook to muzzle those of their employees who contributed to a JR. Yet that kind of behavior was not general: some editors started a dialogue with the local JR on its "Letters to the Editor" page; a few even sent checks.

The worst resistance often came from the press "proletariat." Not only were many journalists too satisfied, too cynical or too scared to lend a hand, but they sometimes openly took their colleagues to task for "fouling their own nest," for "biting the hand that fed them." JRs were accused of being onslaughts on free enterprise—and even invitations to governmental intervention.

What of campus JRs? In the U.S., universities keep too close to the political and economic elite to wish to antagonize the media. Journalism schools need, not only subsidies, but jobs for their graduates. As for professors, the former journalists among them remain loyal to the industry and the pure academics find day-to-day monitoring contemptible.

Quite a few of the JRs launched by working journalists could have been saved by an alternative weekly or a school of journalism, but they chose to scuttle themselves rather than sacrifice their independence. Journalists had opted to go public with grievances but deemed they were the only ones qualified to criticize. Their JRs rarely blame journalists for incompetence, vanity, flunkiness, superficiality, conformity or an underdeveloped sense of social responsibility.

That self-righteousness is not the only flaw on the pages of JRs. In some cases, the contents were very light. Except in metropolises like New York or Washington, there doesn't seem to be enough violations of ethics to justify that they be exposed every month and years on end. The local JRs were justifiably accused of not always discerning properly between a rhetorical explosion and a serious investigation, newsroom gossip and useful revelations, personal vendettas and legitimate grievances. Moreover, because most JRs were born within a big city daily, they seldom got stories on the other media. Lastly, even the best JRs published articles that were ill-documented, badly structured and written. The problem for the editor of a JR was that by criticizing a piece offered for free he offended one more member of a small community. And JRs themselves would sometimes not respect ethics.

That being said, what strikes most is the excellence of so many articles which required long hours of investigation and writing, sometimes at great risk, with no expected reward.

Press Councils

Originally, the idea was Swedish (1916). It reappeared in 1928 in a report of the International Labor Organization, then in the "Court of Honor" project hatched by the International Federation of Journalists (FIJ) in 1931. The Hutchins Commission picked up the idea of a national council in 1947. And, in 1953, Great Britain set up its Press Council, which was to become a model the world over.

There are almost as many formats as there are press councils. In Canada, for instance, because of the size of the country, they were set up at province level. Councils differ by the circumstances of their birth, their initiators, the number of their members, their procedures, their budget, or their prerogatives. To make the picture clearer, they can be classified as follows.

But a warning first: there are pseudo-councils that include representatives of government: their mission is to gag the newsmedia. Also there are some semi-councils: those are handicapped by the absence of lay members. At best, they were organized jointly by publishers and journalists, as in Germany and Austria. More often, they represent only one group, the publishers in Japan, the journalists in Belgium and Switzerland.

The true councils include media users, for one-third to one-half of the total membership. Ideally, such PCs should use all possible means to improve the press. At least, as the constitution of the late British press council provided, a council is expected:

1. To preserve the established freedom of the British press.

2. To maintain the character of the British press in accordance with the highest professional and commercial standards.

3. To consider complaints about the conduct of the press or the conduct of persons and organisations towards the press; to deal with these complaints in whatever manner might seem practical and appropriate and record resultant action.

4. To keep under review developments likely to restrict the supply of information of public interest and importance.

5. To report publicly on developments that may tend towards greater concentration or monopoly in the press (including changes in ownership, control and growth of press undertakings) and to publish statistical information relating thereto.

6. To make representations on appropriate occasions to the Government, organs of the United Nations and to press organisations abroad.

7. To publish periodical reports recording the Council's work and to review from time to time, developments in the press and the factors affecting them.

Some other councils prescribe a concern for education and research.

Unfortunately, up to now, councils have pursued only two missions at most: (1) help the press in its fight for its freedom; and (2) help the press render accounts to the public. And they often limit themselves to the second. A council should be capable of initiating cases, as an effect of closely monitoring the media. The British Press Council has always refused to do it. One explanation is the lack of funds. A council lessens the power of owners, so they cannot be expected to be very generous. Ideally, money should be coming from many sources: public and private organizations, government agencies, foundations, unions, universities and non-media corporations.

Potentially, councils are the most useful M*A*S, but their record is not good. Most councils were created in the late 1960s and early 1970s. By the late 1990s, either they had vanished like those of Portugal, the Caribbean, Burma or the National News Council in the U.S. Or they had never acquired much influence as those of Austria or the

Netherlands. There were only two councils in Latin America (Chile, Peru), two true councils in Black Africa, and none in the Arab World.

In Europe, several councils have been constituted in the 1980s (Turkey, Belgium) and 1990s (Estonia, Denmark, Catalunya). One has died (Portugal); another, in Britain, deeply changed.[16] All told, there are fewer than thirty-five in operation: not one country in ten has a council—although there are many more democracies than before and many more media, private media.

Where PCs have survived, mainly in the north of Europe and in the former dominions of Britain, they cannot be said to have had a great impact. To what extent have the Danish, German, or Norwegian councils improved the media? Could the Australian council do anything to stop the Murdoch group from controlling 60 percent of the Australian daily press? Did the British council play a part in the newspaper revolution of the 1980s, the collapse of reactionary unions and the birth of new dailies?

In no way should these rather depressing remarks about journalism reviews and press councils be considered the last word on M*A*S. They form but an introduction to the next part of this book, whose purpose is to explain why the M*A*S have not yet developed as much as they should, by listing all the resistance and obstacles they have had to face.

But first, what is the development of M*A*S? My 1998 survey gives an idea of what it is in Western Europe, that region of the globe where media first appeared, where they have reached the greatest expansion, the largest media market in the world, if only because the population is superior to that of the U.S. by over 100 million, the GDP superior by 1,000 billion dollars.

European M*A*S 1998

The survey was conducted in seventeen European countries (including Turkey but not the former soviet satellites) among media experts, professionals, and academics, most of them involved in practical ethics, like ombudsmen or secretaries of press councils. The figures here indicate the percentage of countries in which one or the other reply was given.

---

16. No working journalists among its members. Its sole mission now is to deal with complaints.

1a. Have you perceived an increased interest in media ethics in the 1990s?

No: 5% Some: 45%   Quite a lot: 28%   Much: 22%

1b. Over the last couple of years? Yes: all nations surveyed except one (Greece)

2a. How common is it for an individual medium (e.g., newspaper, broadcast station) to have its own code of ethics?

Unknown: 0   Rare: 45%

Occasional: 50%   Common 5%[17]

2b. Is there a generally accepted code of media ethics?

Yes: 94%   No: one country only

2c. When and by whom was that general code drafted?

Union of journalists: 50%   Press Council: 33%

Both together: 17%

2d. As far as you know, was there, in the drafting of the code, any input from non-journalists?

Yes: 7%   No: 93%

3a. Is there a Press Council in your country?

No: 28%   Yes: 72%

National: 13 councils   Regional: one

3b. Does it include any members from outside the media?

Yes: 70%   No: 30%

4a. Have you heard of any local press councils (i.e., liaison committees of newspeople and members of the community)?

Yes: 0%   No: 100%

4b. Have you heard of (non-regular) meetings of members of the local media and of members of the community in a given town to discuss media issues?

No: 53%   Very rare: 17%   Some: 30%

4d. Have you heard of liaison committees set up by media and some group with which they may occasionally clash (e.g., police, magistrates, ethnic minority)?

Yes: 12%   Rare: 30%   No: 53%

---

17. Portuguese law makes it an obligation for newspapers.

5a. Are there any media ombudsmen?
 Yes: 55%   No: 45%
5b. How many: average number per country: 4 to 5.
5d. Have you heard of "ethics coaches" used in newsrooms to raise awareness of and stimulate debate on ethics?
Yes: 18% (only one in 2 of the 3 countries)   No: 82%

6a. Does any medium send questionnaires to people who have been mentioned in the news, to find out if they feel they have been treated with accuracy and fairness?   No: 100%
6b. Does any newspaper print such questionnaires asking the general public what they think about the accuracy and fairness of news treatment?   No: 100%
6c. Do print media regularly do (or commission) surveys to discover what their customers think of their services?
Yes (but rarely): 65%   No: 35%
6e. Is any non-commercial research done on media and media performance by
University research centers: 94%   Foundation-funded think tanks: 47%
Media observatories: 53%   Media foundations: 35%

7a. Do media publish corrections of their mistakes?
All: 23%   Many: 35%   Some: 41%   None: 6%
7b. Do at least most print media do it?
Yes: 60%   No: 40%
7c. The corrections made are usually....
Visible: 47%   Discreet: 53%

8a. Do most print media have "letters to the editor" sections?
All: 47%   Many: 41%   Few or none: 12%
8b. How large are those sections in general?
Less than 1/4 page: 25%   1/2 page: 69%   Full page: 6%
8c. Do they often publish letters critical of their activities?
Yes: 78%   No or very rarely: 22%
8d. Have you heard of media having an on-line message board?
No: 17%   A few: 47%   Some or many: 35%
8g. Do media regularly publish opposite views on the same public issue?
Yes: 89%   No: 11%

9a. Are there any "in-house critics?"
No: 76%   A few: 24%   Many: 0%
9b. Do media publish self-criticism on a regular basis?
None: 50%   Few: 44%   Many: 6%
9c. Are there any (Japanese style) in-house commissions that scruti-
nize and evaluate the contents of the medium?
None: 76%   A few: 24%   Many: 0%
9d. Are there any in-house panels of journalists to review newsroom
issues?
None: 60%   A few: 27%   Many: 13%

10a. Are there any "media reporters" monitoring one or several sectors of the media world and writing critically about them (but NOT
the film critic kind)?
None: 12%   A few: 88%   Many: 0%
10c. Are there any periodicals devoted mainly to media criticism?
Yes: 47%   No: 53%
10e. Are there any radio programs devoted *mainly* to media criticism?
No: 50%   A few: 50%   Many: 0%
10f. Are there any television programs mainly devoted to media criticism?
No: 53%   A few: 47%   Many: 0%

11a. Are there any television series (made locally) that deal with the
media world (like the U.S. *Lou Grant* or *Murphy Brown*)?
No: 72%   A few: 28%   Many: 0%
11b. Can you cite the title (and if possible author and publisher) of a
recently published book devoted to media ethics?
Yes: 81%   No: 19%

12. Have unions of journalists (or of broadcast producers) manifested
an interest in media ethics?
Yes: 95%   No: 5% (one country)

13. Are there media owned, or partly owned, by their own staff?
No: 44%   Very few: 44% A few: 12%

14a. Is further education commonly available for journalists?
Yes: 82%   No: 18%

14b. In the shape of ....
Regular courses: 80%   One-week seminars: 73%
One-day workshops: 87%   Semester/ year-long fellowships: 53%
14c. On average, approximately what proportion of journalists hold a college degree? Estimates range from 10 to 90%; most stand between 30 and 70%
14d. Same question regarding persons entering the profession now? Estimates range from 60 to 80%

15b. Does any general association of consumers pay attention to media products as they do to refrigerators or bank services?
Yes: 6% (one country)   No: 94%
15e. Are there any associations of media consumers?
Yes: 61%   No: 39%
15f. Do these associations all focus on broadcasting?
Yes: 73%   No: 27%
15h. Have you heard of consumers buying stock in a media company so as to have some say at shareholders' meetings?
Yes: 0%   No: 100%

No such survey has been made in the U.S. To ensure that not too many M*A*S be missed, it would probably have to consist of fifty different surveys done at State level. What is known is that in 1999, there were only thirty newspaper ombudsmen in the U.S., three regional press councils (Minnesota, Hawaii, Washington State), and half a dozen journalism reviews.

France, halfway between the north and the south of Europe, a champion of European unity, with the second largest population on the continent and second largest economy, still proud of its pioneering role in the eighteenth century on behalf of human rights, not having undergone peacetime loss of press freedom for over a century, is an interesting area within the new super-power being born. How are the M*A*S doing there?

M*A*S in the French Press

In 1998, I did another survey, this time of the editors of the largest newspapers in the French Regional Daily Press (PQR) to ascertain the use of one or other of the M*A*S by the publication—or its presence in its area of distribution. Two-thirds of the editors responded, 22 out of 32. They were asked if they used any of the M*A*S or had heard about some existing in their part of the country.

Correction boxes: 64%, and other forms of mea culpa: 50%.

"Letters to the editor," by telephone, fax, mail: 95%; or e-mail: 27% .

"Opinion advertising," as when a company or an ideological group buys space or airtime to express views somehow critical of media: 5% (= 1 newspaper).

Accuracy and fairness questionnaires, occasionally mailed to people mentioned in news stories: 14%, or published for all readers to fill out: 14% (= 3 newspapers).

Internal memos by which newsroom executives remind the staff of the principles of good journalism: 82%, or of house rules: 86%.

Code of ethics, internal, drafted by the journalists: 18%, or by management but endorsed by the professionals: 59% .

Regular media pages, including criticism of media: 14%.

Local "journalism reviews," devoted (almost) entirely to information about the media and criticism of their activities: 9%.

Critical books, or reports commissioned by public or private institutions, written by experts, on the behavior of media: 5%.

Small militant media, political party bulletins, alternative newspapers, private non-commercial FM stations, etc.: 23%.

Media reporter, breaking the media tradition of not dealing with media news and issues: 0%.

In-house critic, an individual (as in the U.S.) or a committee (as in Japan) whose reports are not published: 9%.

Ethics coach, an outside expert or an "ethics committee" made up of reporters from the newsroom itself: 14%.

Ombudsman, who listens to angry readers/listeners/viewers, investigates the complaint and publishes, or does not publish, his conclusions: 18% (= 4 newspapers).

Liaison committee, which builds a bridge to whatever group in the population (e.g., the police, an ethnic minority) with which journalists might clash, at the expense of public interest: 0%.

Local press council, i.e., regular meetings of media decisionmakers with representatives of the community so that grievances can be aired: 9% (= 2 newspapers).
Quite similar: a *"panel of customers,"* representative citizens whom the medium questions on their opinions of its services: 9%.

NGO linked to media (e.g., union, professional association, foundation) that occasionally does tests of media quality: 5% (= 1 newspaper).

Association of media users, local or chapter of a national organization, whose aim is an improvement of media: 5%.

Discipline committee, local, of a professional association or union of journalists: 0% .

"Société de rédacteurs," association of a medium's journalists which owns shares in the firm's capital and strives to have "a voice in the product": 14%.

"Société d'usagers," association of the users of some medium which buys shares in its capital to try and have a say in the running of it: 0%.

Media Observatory which scientifically researches media behavior and publishes its findings: 5%.

Higher education: when a journalist is being hired, is it considered important that he/she has university degrees: Yes: 73%; degrees in journalism: Yes: 91%.

Seminars and conferences (a day or two) to update expert knowledge, or raise consciousness—within the firm: 50%, or outside: 36%.

Continuous education (courses or internships, one month to a year) enabling a journalist to acquire or improve his/her expertise in a given field: 77%.

Media in education: teaching in schools on how media function and how they should be used: 73%.

Paying attention to media users, listening sessions (face-to-face or on the phone) in the newsroom, a press club, or elsewhere: 41%.

Opinion research, commercially motivated but the effect of which can be that of a M*A*S: 41%.

Ethical audit which enables a medium to check its ethical standing: 0%.

Non-profit research: campus-based in-depth study that can bring to light long-term omissions and distortions, or again evaluate media effects: 0%.

Some answers are intriguing. Three newspapers, for instance, say they use "accuracy and fairness questionnaires," a M*A*S which is simple, inexpensive. and efficient, but extremely rare in any country. Even taking into account a possible misunderstanding of certain terms in the questionnaire, with which, alas, editors and publishers are not very familiar, the conclusion is clear: M*A*S suffer from underdevelopment in the French provincial press. Admittedly, in small or medium-size countries, some M*A*S normally operate at the national level (like scientific research, journalism reviews, or even press councils), but in France, three-quarters of dailies sold belong to the provincial press. Within that press, the larger dailies, being richer, could afford more easily than others to set up various kinds of M*A*S.

7

Criticisms and Obstacles

Media ethics has developed within vast and complex systems, media and human society: that one point marxist mediologists were right to underline. As a consequence, ethics endures copious and contradictory criticism and must face obstacles all the more stubborn as largely mythical. And so M*A*S are still very much underdeveloped.

Criticisms

Strictures on Codes

It is sometimes claimed that a medium's code of ethics can be used against it in court. It is mentioned as a possibility in the German code. It has happened in the Ivory Coast and Ireland. In the U.S., newspaper lawyers advise their clients not to adopt a code: they fear the local passion for litigation, especially libel suits.

Actually, a code can persuade a jury of the good faith of a respectable medium. Besides, the big media corporations can afford to keep a court case alive until they win it or the plaintiff gives up. Codes, and other M*A*S in their wake, should enable the non-rich and non-powerful to be heard by the media, without going to court.

Another common accusation is that the codes, even though they are mere sheets of paper, threaten press freedom. That could be regarded as a hysterical reaction ... or a tactic to guarantee that no restriction,

---

1. For instance, the wild protests against the project of a code of ethics drafted by the Council of Europe (not the European Parliament) in 1994.

even moral, will be brought to the freedom of making money. But in the 1990s, Scandinavian parliaments did consider the possibility of converting codes into law, once they had been adopted by media professionals. Only Denmark actually did it. Such legalization can solve the problem of enforcing the rules, but it strikes at the very heart of the concept of ethics and self-regulation.

One serious criticism: codes are nothing but lists of vague prohibitions and utopian wishes. Whoever has watched television in the U.S., cannot believe his/her eyes when reading the old NAB code. Similarly, if you compare the journalistic codes of the USSR with what used to be Soviet reality, you wonder whether you should laugh or weep.

In some codes, you find sentences that are devoid of meaning or justification. "The function of a journalist is to tell the truth" sounds beautiful but what is truth? Trillions of true facts are never reported, and quite rightly too. "The public is entitled to know the truth": what is the foundation of such a right? Or again, "the public has a right to be informed": does that mean the right to a photograph of President Kennedy's former wife walking nude on a Greek island beach?

Besides, codes seem to reflect the world vision of journalists, i.e., mainly men, college graduates, urban, decently paid (in the developed world). They tend to leave out the concerns of women, the poor, ethnic minorities. This is even more obvious outside the West, as in India, where journalists are Westernized and often belong to a higher caste; or in Korea, where only 5 percent are women.

In any case, what is the use of a code if it "has no teeth?" When associations, guilds, and unions, after adopting a code, provide for sanctions (e.g., exclusion), these are seldom used. As will be seen infra, the media world is not enthusiastic about M*A*S. Both media owners and journalists need a good deal of public hostility and some governmental growling to start thinking about code enforcement, through a press council, for instance.

Lastly, what is the use of a code if it does not take power relationships into account? There are charters which posit that a journalist should not accept assignments contrary to ethics. An individual will find such rules difficult to respect, especially during a recession. Only top-notch journalists can afford to sacrifice a good job to a non-crucial rule of behavior. It seems indispensable that journalists armor-plate their codes by obtaining more autonomy, by obtaining a share in the editorial management of their publication, or by getting their professional rights spelled out in hiring contracts, or by getting some clauses of the code included in a officialized professional status. In France since 1935, the legal "clause de conscience" allows a journalist to leave his job with his redundancy and other allowances if there is a change in the management or the orientation of the medium which makes it impossible for him/her, in conscience, to continue working there.

Criticism from Left and Right

At neither extremes of the political spectrum is press freedom appreciated. Of course, ethics and M*A*S are despised as ridiculous inventions of naive democrats. To protect either "the nation," or "the people," what you need is to control the media, either by police force, in a fascist regime, or by owning them all, in a communist one.

Disciples of Marx, or of the Frankfurt School, or of the cultural-critical movement, seem to regard media users as puppets manipulated by a few billionaires. The latter, who own most media or give them most of their advertising revenues, supposedly can dictate the contents. The credibility of such critics has suffered much from the fact that, at least before 1991, they forgot ever to turn their critical eye eastward, onto the most widespread of non-capitalist press regimes, the Soviet one.

On the ultra-liberal side, where all media laws and regulations are considered superfluous, ethics is presented as a communist plot against freedom of speech and free enterprise. The journalist has a right to be irresponsible: only his/her conscience is to guide him/her. If a medium does not serve the public, they say, you can trust the market to get rid of it.

Criticism of Realists and Cynics

The real world is so complex, situations are bound to be so diverse, that general rules cannot be of any use or special rules cannot provide for every possible case. A code is inevitably too vague—while the mass of a press council's judgments, after a few years, is too vast. The reporter in a hurry cannot go and look through a book of rules when he/she has to make a decision. Anyway, newspeople don't always agree among themselves about what should be done.

The enforcement of the rules demands that everyone involved apply oneself to it systematically. Users are unorganized, believe they are powerless, do not know the media world well. A media owner has much else to do: primarily, keep his/her firm alive and make it prosper. It should be noted that big media are usually more ethical than the little ones: they are richer and more independent both in relation to the public and to the advertisers.

As for the journalist, serving the public is not his/her only purpose in life: quite naturally, he/she seeks influence, fame, promotion, money. In poor democracies like India or Russia, most journalists cannot bother about ethics: they are too busy keeping their job and raking in a few shekels—or many if they have access to corruption. In many countries of Latin America, most newspeople could not keep body and soul together without a second (or even a third) job, often with an advertiser or a potential newssource. Even in wealthy Western democracies, to thrive (or merely survive) in the profession, one must do favors and yield to friendly pressure.

Criticism by Media Controllers

Some of them genuinely feel a responsibility towards the public. Others have realized that quality control pays. Nevertheless, for many, the law is enough. Any M*A*S is a trespass on their property: who owns the ball sets the rules. If ever a citizen does not like what he/she is being served, let him/her buy another newspaper or switch channels. When such bosses approve of a M*A*S, it is to include it in their PR strategy.

A possibility is that media managers, public or private, are unenthusiastic about M*A*S because, not altogether wrongly, they read in them the sign of an evolution: a slow move towards a participation of producers and consumers (newspeople and public) in media control.

Criticism by Professionals

Today, journalists do not adopt a uniform attitude: some are totally indifferent to ethics and some hypersensitive. In 1994, when the APME asked its membership what they thought of a new version of its 1975 code—more elaborate, precise, and strict—39 percent were favorable, 36 percent totally opposed. Some opponents, especially older journalists, consider self-regulation as merely cosmetic, meant to freshen up the image of media, to trick the public. Or again, they see it as the governmental camel's nose under the media tent.

Most of the stars, the 100 to 200 journalists who, in any country rule the roost because they rub elbows with the major decisionmakers, believe they stand above such concerns. They exploit their position for the money (a lot of money) and influence—and they assert that his/her conscience is quite sufficient to guide a professional.

The Obstacles

Ethics, or quality control, is not a simple and global solution to all media problems, to say the least. If it was an easy panacea, you would see M*A*S everywhere. In fact, there are few in operation. In the only country where almost all have existed, the U.S., many have not survived and most did not multiply. In 1999, there were only about thirty ombudsmen in the country for 1,600 dailies, 7,500 weeklies, 12,000 radio stations and 1,500 television stations, and 2,000 consumer magazines. And yet most have given satisfaction.

That underdevelopment is due to the resistance the M*A*S have met. In no profession is novelty appreciated, especially when it imperils the power or the prestige of people. Among the obstacles to quality control: ignorance, incomprehension, but also, more serious, the nature of man and the nature of M*A*S.

Unjustified Objections

The Threat of Governmental Take-over. A fear is often expressed, especially in the U.S., the fear that the State will use self-control mechanisms to restrict freedom of expression. For instance, it might turn a press council into a Star Chamber.[2] Yet that fear has never been justified, even in India where the press council was set up by law: it is interesting that when Prime Minister Indira Gandhi proclaimed a state of emergency (1975-1977), one of the three press measures she took was to suppress the press council.

Uselessness. Some people insist that "good" media do not need quality control: the staff has always done it as a matter of course. As for

---

2.   Arbitrary tribunal made infamous by James I and Charles I of England.

the "bad" media, they will not accept it: they will not adopt internal M*A*S and will refuse any external institution: The British Press Council was slowly destroyed by an exceptionally unethical popular press, which later accepted the Press Complaints Commission only because it feared Parliament would set up a statutory council. Such arguments are valid, except that most media and most journalists are neither all good nor all bad: they need maps, guidelines, and hand-rails.

The PR Stigma. Supposedly, any effort of the media to control quality is a sham. Media pretend to care about public service while their passion remains maximum profit and (for some) propaganda. Admittedly, the Peoria press council (see p.118) was set up and managed by the PR service at the newspaper. But what seems strange is that a successful commercial formula was not imitated elsewhere. And strange that other M*A*S are so few in spite of the fact that wherever they were used, the public welcomed them.

Partisan Hostility. According to a few critics, ethics is but a mask worn by anti-media activists, mostly from the radical left. Of course, in a conservative society, most of the censors of the status quo are bound to belong to the progressive side. But even in the U.S., some of the most virulent critics stand on the right, like Accuracy in Media (AIM) which, since the early 1970s, has denounced what it claims to be the left-wing slant of U.S. big media, in periodicals, ads and radio programs. In fact, when a M*A*S includes members of the public, experience shows that they never are systematically anti-media.

Ignorance. This obstacle could easily be swept aside. Everyone has heard about ethics, but within and without the media world, most people have simply never heard about the many quality control systems that have been invented, tested, and proved to be efficient and harmless. The media are to blame for that ignorance: they have made no effort to find out about the M*A*S and they have refused to publicize their activities: for instance, the *St. Louis Post-Dispatch*, in spite of its liberal reputation, never mentioned the *St. Louis Journalism Review* for about twenty years. Up to recently, most media even refused to discuss ethics.

True Obstacles

The Dependence of Journalists. Except if he/she is a celebrity, hence precious for his/her employer, a professional must obey orders to obtain publication, to get a salary raise or a promotion. In the Third World, and in wealthy countries with unemployment, journalists cannot afford to endanger their jobs. Unless they are well-protected by law, well-organized, or well-supported by the public, they cannot for ethical reasons antagonize their employers.

Conservatism. The largest French journalists' union, SNJ, in a 1990 White Paper on Media Ethics stigmatized "the old guild-like conservative knee-jerk reactions of a profession that claims for itself a universal right to criticize but would escape any kind of questioning because of its self-bestowed kind of priesthood." Media people do not like change more than anybody else. So, for them to reform themselves, a strong pressure must be exerted, and even threats. Quite often, only the fear of a State legislative intervention convinces media owners and professionals to preempt the move by self-regulation.

Clannishness. The journalistic profession fights back any attack from the outside, which is not surprising. But it seems to be the only one not to have set up so few means of self-discipline. The director general of a big French magazine had this to say in 1993 about the "Affaire Villemin"[3]: "The press does not have to feel ashamed of what it did. Reporters did their job. And we should not pass judgment on ourselves." In the U.S., one gets the same reaction about the Simpson or the JonBenet Ramsey cases. Dog does not eat dog: it is still rare for media to criticize each other, as it is for journalists. In this profession, as in others, solidarity sometimes verges on collusion. Omerta protects the guilty. They are not denounced to management and they rarely go before the disciplinary committees of professional associations. It has been suggested that the traditional antagonism towards M*A*S was to be compared to the collective reaction of bureaucrats, typical of large corporations. They cannot tolerate the intrusion of the public into their microcosm.

---

3. After a little boy was murdered, his father shot a relative whom he accused of being the murderer. Then the mother was suspected. For some reason, this trivial (and still unsolved) case caught the attention of the press which for years hounded all the people involved.

Love of Power. Both the media owner and the professional know, or think, that they wield power. They love the notions of Fourth Estate, of "newsocracy" or "imperial media" and believe they can influence, if only by not publishing information. And they do not wish to share that privilege.

Arrogance. Whether they are competent and courageous or not, professionals think they are. Some who have acquired a reputation refuse to admit that they make mistakes, especially when they are pointed out by a member of the public who, in their view, knows little, understand nothing, and surely has an ax to grind. The FIJ (International Federation of Journalists) has not amended the conclusion of its Bordeaux Declaration of 1954: "A journalist, in professional matters, will accept only the judgment of his peers to the exclusion of any intrusion, governmental *or other*." Any external intervention is regarded as a violation of the sanctuary where, as high priests of information, they follow their calling. Actually, they accept criticism by their peers hardly better: what authority, what superior grace grants those individuals the right to stand in judgment? Journalists it is, most often, who oppose the introduction of an ombudsman in the newsroom.

Press councils sometimes cannot get their pronouncements published. The quality Montreal daily *Le Devoir* even left the Quebec press council after it voted to disapprove of some action by the newspaper. An attitude which turns out to be normal, unfortunately, is expressed in the following statement by one of the top editors of an elite Paris newspaper: "I do not acknowledge the right of anyone outside the newspaper to tell me what I am entitled to do or not to do." Facing the complexity of the real world, one would expect humility to be required, especially as journalists are not often great experts in the field they deal with.

Hyper-susceptibility. As President Truman once said, "If you can't stand the heat, stay out of the kitchen." Yet media people, who have chosen to work in the limelight and some of whom constantly thrash government and business leaders, find it extremely hard to put up with criticism. Some apparently suffer from a fragile ego, possibly because it has swollen out of proportion, as an effect of socializing with VIPs. Since journalists quite commonly disparage the profession and even themselves in private, one is led to wonder if the touchy vanity of journalists might not conceal an inferiority complex. Their consequent fear of ridicule would explain the pack-spirit, the negativism, the cynicism rampant in the profession.

Cost. The last two obstacles to the creation of M*A*S are very concrete: contrary to the ones just mentioned, they cannot be dispelled simply by training, negotiation. or experience. First of all, many (though not all) are expensive, to operate and to publicize.

An ombudsman, for instance, needs to be an experienced and highly respected journalist, hence a very well-paid employee. A press council crucially needs to obtain enough money to function fast,[5] contrary to law courts. Enough money also to assume all its functions, not just that of umpire—and to let it be known that it is assuming them.

As only a fraction of the money needed can come from the State, little quality control can be done without financing by media owners, and they are quite reluctant to pay. While a M*A*S does not in any way threaten their income (very much to the contrary), it does threaten their power: it gives the public a voice and tends to strengthen the autonomy of the journalistic staff.

The M*A*S represent an excellent investment. All big business firms spend fortunes to improve the image which the public, the government, and the courts have of them. A few years back, they discovered the appeal of ethics, yet many media had rather buy technical equipment or increase dividends than spend on M*A*S.

And then some media do not have the money to spare. "Social responsibility" then is quite a tough act. Some newspapers, for instance, cannot afford to forbid their reporters from accepting a trip offered by some corporation. The founder-editor of a famous French daily recommended that journalists accept the junket and then, as the French say, "spit in the soup," i.e., bad-mouth the company or institution that paid for it. That is an option but not very elegant and fraught with ambiguity.

Time. The worst of the obstacles assumes a double shape. On the one hand, quality control consumes time, which is always in short supply in the media world. On the other hand, it functions on a long-term basis: the best method is education which bears fruit only after many

---

5.   The late British Press Council took 8 to 12 months to adjudicate a complaint.

years. Moreover, most M*A*S require that professionals and public get used to them, which takes a long while.

A Fundamental Flaw. None of the M*A*S is perfect. To take just a few, the press council is too complex, the code too soft, the ombudsman too expensive, education too slow. But those drawbacks pale to insignificance compared to a deep flaw of ethics: it can—in the U.S. it often does—divert attention from those that truly determine the behavior of media. Major decisions are naturally taken at the top, not by the rank and file. The dominant criterion used is economic, not moral. In other words, the important responsibilities are not in the hands of journalists.

It is undoubtedly immoral for a reporter to kill a story in exchange for a bribe. But what of a radio station which would rather increase its profits than hire the extra reporter it needs to cover the local news properly? Certainly it is contrary to ethical rules for journalists to accept presents and other favors. But what of media that seduce advertisers by promising to support their ads with editorial material written for that purpose?

Take the major press scandal of the early 1980s: Janet Cooke, of the *Washington Post*, won a Pulitzer prize for a series on a character that she, in fact, had invented, Jimmy, an 8-year-old heroin addict. This was contrary to ethics but probably she yearned to get her byline on the front page, a promotion, a prize. She knew what would please: an exceptional human interest story. And what would not please: one more report on poverty and drugs in the black ghettos. She lied—but before passing judgment on her, one should remember those hundreds of fat U.S. media which for years ignored famine and epidemics in black Africa because correspondents are expensive and, mainly, because they know their customers do not give a damn for the Third World.

It is not right to invade the privacy of a grieving family, to treat all women as bimbos or housewives, or to distort the meaning of a speech by inaccurate quotes: those are some of the issues discussed in seminars on ethics. Faults of that type, which reporters commit, are very visible for the reader or viewer. Put together, they do add up to a regrettable pile. But as breaches of public service, can such violations of ethics decently be compared to the transgressions of media companies? When, for instance, those companies impede the development of new technologies for decades to protect their oligopoly on earlier media, as was the case in the U.S.with FM, UHF, and cable television. Or when they omit all news that might irritate their advertisers or other business circles.

A firm can hardly be moral or immoral for lack of a conscience. What it can do, however, is to make it possible for its employees to respect ethical rules. It is better that a reporter check his/her facts: does his/her station give him/her access to data banks? It is better that a reporter do not accept free tickets to a play or game that he/she will review, but will the newspaper accept to buy a ticket?

Between the antisocial behavior of journalists and of firms, the difference of scale is sometimes so great that the discussion of ethics may sound rather futile. Indeed, it could turn dangerous. Might it not be part of a strategy aiming at, first, giving newspeople the illusion of being true professionals (while they cannot be so for lack of independence and funds). Then, second, shifting the dissatisfaction of the public onto them, and sending them out into the wilderness, like the proverbial scapegoats?

Conclusion

Media all over the planet have greatly improved in the last fifty years. First because of the new means of communication: among other effects, the "technologies of freedom"[1] make censorship of speech almost impossible for dictators of any stripe. On the other hand, the control of the media world by huge corporations has increased. Professionals and public need to get mobilized, organized, and to furnish themselves with the needed equipment and weapons. Already, over the last half century, much of the improvement has been due to their action. For instance, it was popular pressure that led European governments to lift the State monopoly on broadcasting in the 1980s.

A New Environment

It is usually in times of crisis that media start worrying about ethics.[2] Then, alas, they tend to regard it only as a tool for Public Relations, which could be very dangerous for their prosperity and their future. Today, fortunately, deep forces are at work. First factor: the slow rise of the level of knowledge and activism in the public. More people are becoming aware that good media services are crucial; that media should fulfill *all* their missions; that traditional media are not satisfactory . And very slowly, they are growing conscious that they must take part in the reform. A second factor seems to be the better perception that young professionals have of their calling and the greater passion some bring to the fight for the freedom and responsibility of media.

Quality control is becoming both more useful and feasible. More feasible because more and more nations have established press free-

---

1. *Technologies of Freedom* was the title of a book by Ithiel de Sola Pool, Cambridge, Harvard University Press, 1983.
2. Thus, in 1989, fearing a law that would create a "right of reply," British national quality dailies drafted a charter and appointed ombudsmen.

dom,[3] and State monopoly on broadcasting has disappeared almost everywhere. Besides, M*A*S have become more useful for two reasons. First, because of the growing menace of Mammon over the media. In the past, it has been made clear that news and new ideas can be blocked out if they threaten the interests of big corporations. And, second reason, the new technology shows an alarming flip side: it makes invasion of privacy far easier; live reports go on the air with no checking, filtering, or pondering; on the Internet, the distribution of Nazi propaganda or pathological pornography has become commonplace.

Quality Pays

Media ethics, of course, is one element in a wider movement of progress: improvement in the gathering of information, in the competence of staff, in picture and color quality, in layout, printing, distribution, etc. Such an evolution eventually benefits everybody, owners, advertisers, professionals, technicians, and the public. Quality can serve both the welfare of mankind and the bottom line.

In the U.S., under the slings and arrows of criticism, some media proprietors wish to serve the public better. Many feel the financial need for it. Commercial television loses the more educated and wealthy viewers, to the grief of advertisers. The printed press feels the competition of newer media, and the newspaper keeps losing its readers even in the absence of any rival. Furthermore, some owners are becoming aware that they risk forfeiting their lucrative freedom: the executive or the legislative power, ever inclined to shackle the press, will do it with a wonderfully democratic pretext, the dissatisfaction of the public.

Another problem is rarely mentioned, a trend towards the proletarization of journalists: in the U.S. real salaries decline, everywhere morale is declining. This is linked to the use of the rank and file as pawns by profit-oriented media. Ethics can help for it increases the protection of journalists, their solidarity, their prestige, their influence—hence their morale, hence their productivity. As for the public, ethics will directly increase its enjoyment and will ultimately increase its trust in the media.

---

3. The first newspaper ombudsman in Europe was appointed by *El Pais*, the great Spanish daily born just after the end of the Franco dictatorship.

the British popular daily press has lost about 4 million customers over the last fifty years while the population increased by more than 7 million. Is it not interesting that when a U.S. television station decided, after the year-long media obsession with the worthless Simpson case, not to mention crime any more except when it was in the public interest—it saw its ratings climb immediately. Movies without violence, or vulgarity, or obscenity are doing very well at the box-office, which Hollywood seems to have trouble registering. *Schindler's List,* which made a lot of money, would not have been filmed if Spielberg himself had not underwritten the financial risk. In a totally different environment, in the post-Soviet Latvia of the 1990s, an ethical behavior became a way for a newspaper of distinguishing itself in the free-for-all of corrupt media and of thus surviving.

Ethics and M*A*S, it should be remembered, have several purposes: improve the services of media to the public; restore the prestige of media in the eyes of the population; diversely protect freedom of speech and press; obtain, for the profession, the autonomy that it needs to play its part in the expansion of democracy and the betterment of the fate of mankind.

The Autonomy of Professionals

The number one target of professionals must be, not to increase the revenues of the firm they work for, but to serve better the various minorities that make up their public. Being employees they cannot openly oppose their employers. How can they escape their dependence? The best way is to do their job like first-class craftsmen: to excel in the observation of events and trends, in the interviewing of decisionmakers, in the organization of data, in the explanation of facts and ideas, in the phrasing of stories. Their excellent products will provide their bosses (and, most probably, thousands of share-holders) with abundant revenues, which should keep them happy.

On the other hand, by always behaving according to the principles and rules of the profession, by providing the public with unimpeachable journalistic services, by being diversely accountable to it, newspeople will earn the support of citizens for the media as an industry, for the Fourth Estate as an institution, and for themselves as expert gatherers and processors of information. If ever unjustified pressure was put on them, then journalists could resist by sheltering in their professionalism. Their interest for ethics can be interpreted as a sign that they intend eventually to take over at least some of the levers of power.

Freedom and Quality

Nowadays in most Western countries at least a fraction of the professionals has understood that quality control was for them an excellent operation to counter the frantic commercialization of media. They have understood that systems like the M*A*S satisfied media consumers by giving them access, that consequently M*A*S increased the influence and prestige of the profession. Some journalists have realized that far from threatening their freedom M*A*S made a remarkable weapon, maybe the absolute weapon, to *protect* media freedom against all its enemies.

Ethics Not Enough

The obvious improvement of media over the last half century may seem due mainly to electronics, to the end of State monopoly on broadcasting, or to obligations imposed on media by the State. True it is that on the ethical side evolution goes only at glacier speed. In a historical perspective, however, changes can be perceived: gone are the blackmail rags, the party dailies, the enslavement of broadcasting to government, the sickening campaigns against individuals or ideas. Fewer are the envelopes in the hands of journalists, more numerous the university degrees.

Overestimating ethics, however, would be just as dangerous as underestimating it. In today's world, after the collapse of the communist block, the main threat to the freedom and quality of media consists in the frantic exploitation of communication channels by giant profit-oriented firms. No one should dream that their greed can be curbed by ethics. When the Berlin Wall fell, it crushed the claims of the champions of sovietized media. But on the other side, the market fanatics are still hard at work. Even if all "quality control systems" were deployed, it would not be enough.

There will always be a need for laws and regulations. First to ensure a level playing field for all media. Secondly, to restrain the natural trend of commercial firms towards concentration, maximum profit, and ensuing neglect of public service. Lastly, because a journalist is not responsible alone for all that goes right or wrong in the media. Is it not absurd to think that the media would be rid of their flaws if only their personnel became ethical? Yet that claim is not uncommon in Anglo-Saxon countries where salvation is expected to come from a combination of market and ethics.

Europeans, while freeing the audiovisual media from the governmental yoke in the 1980s, have very reasonably preserved a relatively strict regulation to protect the public interest—and developed more and more of an interest in ethics. In fact, society needs all three: the law, the market and quality control. The proportion of each ingredient in the blend is hard to determine: it will be influenced by the local culture and historical accidents.

What Remains to Be Done

There exists an excellent U.S. political concept, that of "moral leadership." It consists in setting a noble goal to a nation, social group, or institution, while knowing full well that it cannot immediately be reached. It consists in persuading people of the rightness of the quest, in convincing them to work in the good direction, without illusions but with faith. Preaching the gospel of ethics and M*A*S partakes of "moral leadership."

One should remember the radical Protestants of mid-seventeenth-century England. Among the demands they made was the right to education, to health, to work—for all. Free and compulsory education, a national health system, and unemployment benefits that seemed crazily utopian in those days, have become commonplace.

Networks of M*A*S

Is it enough that sensitive, smart or striking words be uttered in workshops, seminars, conferences, in articles, books, broadcast programs? Should we be content with codes that will never be enforced? No. Hence the M*A*S. At this point in time, it would be absurd to start debating the worth of them. As was said before, they have all been tried and have proved they could be efficient and, at their worst, harm no one.

The aim now must be to attract the attention of professionals and the public on that accumulated experience and on the great potentiali-

The aim now must be to attract the attention of professionals and the public on that accumulated experience and on the great potentialities of accountability systems. Since many M*A*S are new on the media stage, nobody is used to them. Admittedly, these nongovernmental non-profit agents should be introduced and developed gradually. A network of M*A*S can only be built slowly, even very slowly at the start.

Why a network? The reason is that while every existing M*A*S is useful, none is sufficient. None can be expected to produce great direct effects. They supplement each other, as they function at different levels and in different time frames. To the extent that they reenforce each other, we can hope for a snowball effect at some time. The big problem is to start the ball rolling. Together, the M*A*S can have a strong long-term influence. The ideal would be that, within a few decades, they all exist everywhere and that they cooperate, without shedding their autonomy, in a vast and flexible web.

Take, for instance, the one that existed temporarily in Minneapolis in the 1970s. The Minnesota News Council had roots in the excellent Journalism School of the university; professors at the school also helped the *Twin Cities Journalism Review* which was produced by local journalists, advised the local daily press and broadcasting stations, set up a Free press/Fair trial committee. They also wrote articles and books,[4] of course, and taught ethics.

Promotion

As it seems agreed that media ethics should be based on free will and consensus, the interested parties need to discuss what precisely the rules are going to be and how they will be enforced. Proselytizing efforts must be aimed both at managers and managed. When the interest in ethics developed, everywhere in the world a concern also appeared to find ways to incite professionals to respect the rules: in almost every part of the planet, people have given the issues some thought, they have written about them, and experimented. So it is necessary that exchanges of information take place between the various regions. Here are a few suggestions, of a practical kind. Their

---

4.   Including a classic: Jo Edward Gerald's *The Social Responsibility of the Press*, Minneapolis, U. of Minnesota Press, 1963.

purpose is to make M*A*S known to media personnel, politicians, and the general public.

Research and Communication

One of the first steps to take should be worldwide research on what has been said and, more importantly, what has been done in the way of media ethics and accountability systems—a field study among persons who work and have worked on quality control. This inventory should be published as one or several books that would present the history, the variety, the social role of M*A*S, as well as the problems they face. The volume should be published in several languages—and one version at least should be concise, attractive, and inexpensive.

There is a need to inform and inform and inform. Meetings should be organized in various parts of the world to excite the interest of journalists, to attract the attention of media, to lead decisionmakers of all kinds into promoting the creation of M*A*S. There have been conferences, seminars, workshops in the 1980s and 1990s, often on the initiative of press councils, or of the Council of Europe. But the International Press Institute (IPI), the World Association of Newspapers (formerly FIEJ), the International Federation of Journalists (FIJ), and other NGOs, even Unesco, could put their shoulders to the wheel. And also, in the U.S., journalism schools, foundations, professional associations, and press groups with a yearning for quality.

Information Centers

In addition, centers of information and communication dedicated to media ethics should be created in several regions of the globe. Within universities, for instance, or foundations or observatories or research institutions concerned by media. One center at least per continent plus web sites with news bulletins, forums, chat lines, and data banks. The first such web site was started, with very modest means, by the Institut français de presse (University of Paris-2) at the beginning of 1999 www. u-paris2.fr/ifp.

The purpose of such centers and sites is to help improve media services without any State intervention. They should have several functions. First, gather information on any crisis of an ethical nature to have taken place in one country or another; on meetings and training fessional ethics. Secondly, they should gather a rich documentation on media ethics and M*A*S: articles, reports, dissertations and theses, old and recent books. Thirdly, they should make that documentation available to the public—by various means (web pages, bibliographical bulletin, microfiches, CD-ROM)—and should answer inquiries by email, fax and mail.

Centers and sites should also promote the exchange of information, experience, and ideas. They should stimulate communication between journalists, radio and television producers, academics, magistrates, politicians, members of the public—on the topics of ethics and accountability by suggesting or actually organizing workshops, round tables, conferences; by publishing a gazette; by copublishing books related to ethics and M*A*S.

Funds should come from the largest possible number of sources so as to insure the independence of the institution, preferably foundations, universities, national and international associations of publishers and of journalists. But the list might be carefully extended to regulatory agencies, television networks, press groups, etc.

Media ethics is not a fad that was born in the U.S. after the protest of the 1960s and in Europe after the Gulf War, the kind of short-lived counterattack to deal with a wave of public distrust, as happened before, as in the 1920s in reaction against the Progressive movement. It is not the fantasy of some intellectuals: the champions of media ethics and M*A*S have little in common with the erudite medieval theologians who fiercely debated issues which bishops, priests, and the faithful knew nothing about and cared for even less. And media ethics is not the strategy of an adman. It is the only method to improve the media that is perfectly democratic and both efficient and harmless. It does act slowly. So there is all the more cause to develop M*A*S with no delay. As any new undertaking, it requires energy, an innovative spirit, devotion, a sense of organization, and a gift for teamwork—plus some investment.

Bibliography

Bibliographies

Christians, Clifford, and Vernon Jensen. *Two Bibliographies on Ethics*, 2nd ed. Minneapolis: University of Minnesota Press, 1988.
Cooper, Thomas W., *Television and Ethics: A Bibliography*. Boston, G.K. Hall, 1988.
MacDonald, Barrie, and Michel Petheram. *Keyguide to Information Sources in Media Ethics*. London, Lansell, 1998.

General Works

Ethics, Business, and the Professions
Andrews, Kenneth R. (ed.). *Ethics in Practice: Managing the Moral Corporation*. Boston MA: Harvard Business School Press, 1989.
Bayles, Michae. *Professional Ethics*. Belmont, CA: Wadsworth, 1981 [general panorama].
Freudberg, David. *The Corporate Conscience: Money, Power and Responsible Business*. New York: American Management Association, 1986.
Jonas, H. *The Imperative of Responsibility: In Search of an Ethics for the Technological Age*. Chicago: University of Chicago Press, 1984.

Ethics and Media

Adams, Julian. *Freedom and Ethics in the Press*. New York: Rosen, 1983.
Beauchamp, Tom L., and Stephen Klaidman. *The Virtuous Journalist*. New York: Oxford University Press, 1987.
Belsey, Andrew, and Ruth Chadwick. *Ethical Issues in Journalism and the Media*. London: Routledge, 1992 [British viewpoint].
Christians, Clifford, Ferre, John P., and Mark P. Fackler. *Good News: Social Ethics and the Press*. New York: Oxford University Press, 1992 [a philosophical approach].
Christians, Clifford, and Michael Traber (eds.). *Communication Ethics and Universal Values*. London: Sage, 1997.
Gordon, A.D., and John M. Kittross. *Controversies in Media Ethics*, 2nd ed. New York: Addison Wesley, 1999.
Haselden, Kyle. *Morality and the Mass Media*. Nashville, TN: Broadman, 1968 [Christian viewpoint].
Iggers, Jeremy. *Good News, Bad News: Journalism Ethics and the Public Interest*. New York: Worldview Press, 1998.
Jaksa, James A. *Communications Ethics*. Belmont CA: Wadsworth, 1988.
Johannesen, Richard L. *Ethics in Human Communication*, (1975), 3rd ed. Prospect Heights IL: Waveland Press, 1990.
Kieran, Matthew. *Media Ethics: A Philosophical Approach*. Westport, CT: Praeger, 1997.
Lambeth, Edmund B. *Committed Journalism: An Ethic for the Profession*, 2nd ed. Bloomington, Indiana University Press, 1992.

Merrill, John C. *Legacy of Wisdom: Great Thinkers and Journalism*. Ames: Iowa State University Press, 1994.

Olen, Jeffrey. *Ethics in Journalism*. Englewood Cliffs, NJ: Prentice-Hall, 1988.

Rivers, William L., and Cleve Mathews. *Ethics for the Media*. Englewood Cliffs, NJ: Prentice-Hall, 1988.

Rubin, Bernard. *Questioning Media Ethics*. New York: Praeger, 1978.

Schwartz, Tony. *The Responsive Chord*. Garden City, NY: Doubleday, 1973 [ethics in broadcasting].

McBride, Sean (ed.). *Many Voices, One World*. Paris: Unesco, 1980.

Van Der Meiden, Anne (ed.). *Ethics and Mass Communication*. Utrecht: State University of Utrecht, 1980.

History (before World War II)

Crawford, Nelson A. *The Ethics of Journalism* New York: Alfred A. Knopf, 1924; new ed. 1969.

Dicken-Garcia, Hazel. *Journalistic Standards in Nineteenth Century America*. Madison: University of Wisconsin Press, 1989.

Flint, Leon N. *The Conscience of the Newspaper: A Case Book in the Principles and Problems of Journalism*. New York: Appleton, 1925.

Kingsbury, Susan M. *Newspaper and the News: An Objective Measurement of Ethical and Unethical Behavior by Representative Newspapers*, (1937). New York: Johnson Reprint Corporation, 1969.

Laws and Regulations

Couprie, Eliane, and Henry Olsson. *Freedom of Communications Under the Law: Case Studies in Nine Countries*. Manchester: European Institute for the Media, 1987.

Curry, J.L., et al. *Press Control Around the World*. New York: Praeger, 1982.

Dewall, Gustav von. *Press Ethics: Regulation and Editorial Practice*. Düsseldorf: European Institute for the Media, 1997 [France, Germany, Italy, Sweden, United Kingdom].

Hoffmann-Reim, Wolfgang. *Regulating Media: The Licensing and Supervision of Broadcasting in Six Countries*. New York: Guilford, 1996.

Robertson, Geoffrey, and Andrew Nicol., *Media Law: The Rights of Journalists, Broadcasters and Publishers*. London: Sage, 1985.

Social Responsibility

Balk, Alfred. *A Free and Responsible Press*. New York: Report to the 20th Century Fund, 1973.

Casebier, Allan, and Janet J. Casebier. *Social Responsibilities of the Mass Media*. Lanham, MD: University Press of America, 1978.

Collins, Keith S. (ed.). *Responsibility and Freedom in the Press: Are They in Conflict?* Washington, DC: Citizen's Choice, 1985.

Commission on the Freedom of the Press. *A Free and Responsible Press*. Chicago: University of Chicago Press, 1947.

Dennis, Everette E., et al. (eds.). *Media Freedom and Accountability*. New York: Greenwood, 1989.

Elliott, Deni (ed.). *Responsible Journalism*. Beverly Hills, CA: Sage, 1986 [nine essays by academics].

Gerald. J. Edward. *The Social Responsibility of the Press*. Minneapolis: University of Minnesota Press, 1963.

Hodges, Louis (ed.). *Social Responsibility: Journalism, Law, Medicine*. Lexington, VA: Washington & Lee University, 1978.

Jonas, Hans. *The Imperative of Responsibility*. Chicago: University of Chicago Press, 1984.

Merrill, John C. *The Imperative of Freedom: A Philosophy of Journalistic Autonomy*. New York: Hastings House, 1974 [Hostile to "social responsibility"].

Merrill, John C., *The Dialectic in Journalism: Toward a Responsible Use of Press Freedom*. Baton Rouge: Louisiana State University Press, 1989.

Rivers, William, W., Schramm, and C. Christians. *Responsibilities in Mass Communication*. New York: Harper & Row, 1957, 3rd ed. 1980.

Schmuhl, Robert (ed.). *The Responsibilities of Journalism*. Notre Dame, IN: University of Notre Dame Press, 1984.

Media Ethics and M*A*S

Media Ethics

Alley, Robert S. *Television: Ethics for Hire?* Nashville, TN: Abingdon, 1977 [based on interviews with eminent producers].

Christians, Clifford et al. *Media Ethics,* 3rd ed. New York: Longman, 1991 [76 case studies].

Day, Louis A, *Ethics in Media Communication: Cases and Controversies*. Belmont, CA: Wadsworth, 1996.

European Journalism Center. *Organising Media Accountability*. Maastricht: EJC, 1997.

Fink, Conrad C. *Media Ethics: In the Newsroom and Beyond*. New York: McGraw Hill, 1988.

Goodwin, Eugene, and R.F. Smith. *Groping for Ethics in Journalism*. Ames: Iowa State University Press, 1983, 3rd ed., 1994.

Heine, W. *Journalism Ethics: A Case Book*. London, Canada: University of Western Ontario, 1975.

Hulteng, John L. *The Messenger's Motives: Ethical Problems of the News Media*. Englewood Cliffs, NJ: Prentice-Hall, 1976, 2nd ed., 1985.

Kieran, Matthew (ed.). *Media Ethics*. London: Routledge, 1998.

Klaidman, Stephen, and Tom L. Beauchamp. *The Virtuous Journalist*. New York: Oxford University Press, 1987 [based on real life situations].

Krieghbaum, Hillier. *Pressures on the Press*. New York: Crowell, 1972.

Lester, Paul. *Photojournalism: An Ethical Approach*. Hillsdale, NJ: Erlbaum, 1991.

Limburg, Val E. *Electronic Media Ethics*. Boston: Focal, 1994.

McCulloch, F. (ed.). *Drawing the Line*. Washington, DC: ASNE, 1984 [How 31 editors solved their worst ethical problem].

Meyer, Philip. *Editors, Publishers and Newspaper Ethics*. Washington, DC: ASNE, 1983.

Meyer, Philip. *Ethical Journalism: A Guide for Students, Practitioners and Consumers*. New York: Longman, 1987 [a classic].

SPG-SDX, National Ethics Committee. *Journalism Ethics Report.* Chicago: Society of Professional Journalists, every year since 1981.

Nordenstreng, Kaarle (ed.). *Reports on Media Ethics in Europe.* Tampere, Finland: University of Tampere, 1995.

Patterson, Philip, and Lee Wilkins. *Media Ethics: Issues and Cases.* Dubuque, IA: William C. Brown, 1991.

Pippert, Wesley G. *An Ethics of News: A Reporter's Search for Truth.* Washington, DC: Georgetown University Press, 1989 [personal experiences].

Russell, Nick. *Morals and Media: Ethics in Canadian Journalism.* University of British Columbia Press, 1994.

Seib, Philip. *Campaigns and Conscience: The Ethics of Political Journalism.* Westport, CT: Praeger, 1994.

Stephenson, Hugh, and Michael Bromley (eds). *Sex, Lies and Democracy.* London: Longman, 1998.

Swain, Bruce M. *Reporters' Ethics.* Ames: Iowa State University Press, 1979 [problems faced by 67 reporters].

Thayer, Lee, et al. (ed.). *Ethics, Morality and the Media.* New York: Hastings House, 1980 [27 essays mainly by practitioners].

Codes

Bruun, Lars (ed.). *Professional Codes in Journalism.* Prague: IOJ, 1979 [IOJ was a soviet institution].

Cooper, Thomas W. (ed.). *Communication Ethics and Global Change.* New York: Longman, 1989.

Gorlin, Rena A. (ed.). *Codes of Professional Responsibility,* 2nd ed. Washington, DC: Bureau of National Affairs, 1990.

IOJ. *International Principles of Professional Ethics in Journalism.* Prague: IOJ, 1986 [see supra: Bruun].

Jones, G. Clement. *Mass Media Codes of Ethics and Councils.* Paris: Unesco, 1980 [strong Marxist bias].

Juusela, Pauli. *Journalistic Codes of Ethics in the CSCE Countries.* Tampere: University of Tampere, 1991 [A synthetic study of Western and Soviet codes!].

Criticism

Aronson, James. *Packaging the News: A Critical Survey of Press, Radio, TV.* New York: International Publishers, 1971.

Aronson, James. *Deadline for the Media: Today's Challenges to Press, TV and Radio.* Indianapolis: Bobbs-Merrill, 1972.

Babb, Laura L. (ed.). *Of the Press, By the Press, For the Press, and Others Too.* Boston: Houghton Mifflin, 1976 [by *Washington Post* staff members].

Brown, Lee. *The Reluctant Reformation: On Criticizing the Press in America.* New York: McKay, 1974.

Cirino Robert, *Don't Blame the People: How the News Media Use Bias, Distortion and Censorship to Manipulate Public Opinion,* New York, Random House, 1971.

Downing, John, et al. *Questioning the Media: A Critical Introduction.* Newbury Park, CA: Sage, 1990.

Franklin, Robert. *Newszak and News Media*. London: Arnold, 1997.

Goldstein, Tom. *The News at Any Cost: How Journalists Compromise Their Ethics to Shape the News*. New York: Simon and Schuster, 1985 [concrete cases].

Goldstein, Tom (ed.). *100 Years of Media Criticism*. New York: Columbia University Press, 1989.

Hachten, William. *The Troubles of Journalism: A Critical Look at What's Right and Wrong With the Press*. Mahwah, NJ: Erlbaum, 1998.

Isaacs, Norman E. *Untended Gates: The Mismanaged Press*. New York: Columbia University Press, 1986.

Jensen, Carl. *20 Years of Censored News*. New York: Seven Stories Press, 1997.

Jensen, Joli. *Redeeming Modernity: Contradictions in Media Criticism*. Newbury Park, CA: Sage, 1990.

MacDougall, A. Kent (ed.). *The Press: A Critical Look From the Inside*, Princeton, Dow Jones, 1972.

Pollak, Richard (ed.). *Stop the Presses, I Want to Get Off!*. New York: Random House, 1975. [An anthology from the review (MORE)].

Rusher, William A. *The Coming Battle for the Media: Curbing the Media Elite*. New York: William Morrow and Co., 1988 [a conservative viewpoint].

Shaw, David. *Journalism Today*. New York: Harper & Row, 1977 [an anthology of his articles in the *Los Angeles Times*].

Shaw, David. *Press Watch: A Provocative Look at How the Newspapers Report the News*. New York: Macmillan, 1984.

Sinclair, Upton. *The Brass Check: A Study of American Journalism*. Pasadena, CA, 1919, reprinted by Arno Press, 1970.

Public Access/ Right to Communicate

Barron, Jerome C. *Freedom of the Press For Whom? The Right of Access to Mass Media*. Bloomington: Indiana University Press, 1973.

Harms, L. S., Jim Richstad, and K.A. Kie (eds.). *Right to Communicate: Collected Papers*. Honolulu: University Press of Hawaii, 1977.

Harms, L. S., and Jim Richstad (eds.). *Evolving Perspectives on the Right to Communicate*. Honolulu: East-West Center, 1977.

Schmidt, Benno C. *Freedom of the Press vs. Public Access*. New York: Praeger, 1976.

Press Councils

Adhikari, G. *Press Councils: The Indian Experience*. New Delhi: Press Institute of India, 1965.

Balk, Alfred. *A Free and Responsive Press: Report for a National News Council*. New York: 20th Century Fund, 1973.

Bradley, H.J. *Press Councils of the World*. London: The Press Council, 1974 [mimeographed].

Brogan, Patrick. *Spiked: The Short Life and Death of the National News Council*. New York: Priority, 1985 [the U.S. national PC].

IPI. *Press Councils and Press Codes*. Zürich: International Press Institute, 1964 and 1967.

Levy, Philip. *The Press Council: History, Procedures and Cases*. London: Macmillan, 1967 [the British Press Council].
Murray, George. *The Press and the Public: The Story of the British Press Council*. Carbondale: Southern Illinois University Press, 1972.
Rivers, William L., et al. *Backtalk: Press Councils in America*. San Francisco: Canfield, 1972 [local PCs in the U.S.].
Trikha, N. K. *The Press Council: A Self-Regulatory Mechanism for the Press*. Bombay: Somaiya Publications, 1986.

University Training and Research

Brislin, Tom (ed.). *Teaching Media Ethics*, special issue of the *Journal of Mass Media Ethics*, Volume 12, 1997.
Christians, Clifford, and Catherine L. Covert. *Teaching Ethics in Journalism Education*, New York, Hastings, 1980.
Ellliott, Deni. *Toward the Development of a Model for Journalism Ethics Instruction*. Ann Arbor, MI: University Microfilms, 1984.
Lemert, James. *Criticizing the Media: Empirical Approaches*. Newbury Park, CA: Sage, 1989.
Sloan, William David (ed.). *Makers of the Media Mind: Journalism Educators and Their Ideas*. Hillsdale, NJ: Erlbaum, 1990.

Other M*A*S

Kessler, Lauren. *The Dissident Press, Alternative Journalism in American History*. Beverly Hills, CA: Sage, 1984.
Maezawa, Takeshi. *Watchdog: A Japanese Newspaper Ombudsman at Work*. Tokyo: Cosmohills, 1994 [in English].
Whitney, D. Charles. *Begging Your Pardon: Corrections and Correction Policies at Twelve US Newspapers*. New York: Columbia University, Gannett Center for Media Studies, 1986.

Major Reviews

American Journalism Review, University of Maryland, 1117 Journalism Building, College Park, MD 20742-7111.
Brill's Content, 521 Fifth Ave, New York, NY 10175.
Columbia Journalism Review, Journalism Building, Columbia University, 2950 Broadway, New York, NY 10027.
Journal of Mass Media Ethics, c/o Erlbaum, 10 Industrial Ave, Mahwah, NJ 07430-2262.
Media Ethics, Division of Mass Communication, Emerson College, 100 Beacon Street, Boston, MA 02116.

A Few Interesting Web Sites

American JR : www.ajr.org
California State U. Fullerton:
www.commfaculty.fullerton.edu/lester/ethics/ethics_list.html; then click on "media eth-
    ics"
University of Tampere, Finland: for the texts of European codes
    www.uta.fi/ethicnet
Columbia JR: www.cjr.org
ONO, world association of news ombudsmen:
    www.infi.net/ono
Poynter Institute: www.poynter.org provides links with many sites touching on media
    ethics
Université de Paris-2, Institut français de presse
    www.u-paris2.fr/ifp (then click on "media ethics"): links with world press councils
    and other sites concerned with media ethics.
University of British Columbia, Centre for Applied Ethics
    www.ethics.ubc.ca/resources/media"

Some Books in French

Alix, François-Xavier. *Une éthique pour l'information*. Paris: L'Harmattan, 1997.
Bernier, Marc-François. *Ethique et déontologie du journalisme*. Québec: Presses de
    l'université Laval, 1994.
Bertrand, Claude-Jean. *La déontologie des médias*. Paris: PUF Que Sais-Je, 1997(2nd
    ed. 1999).
Bertrand, Claude-Jean. L'Arsenal de la démocratie: médias, déontologie el M*A*R*S,
    Paris, Economica, 1999.
Cayrol, Roland. *Médias et démocratie: la dérive*. Paris: Presses de Sciences Po, 1997.
Cornu, Daniel. *Ethique de l'information*. Paris: PUF Que Sais-Je, 1997.
Cornu, Daniel. *Journalisme et vérité: pour une éthique de l'information*. Genève:
    Labor & Fides, 1994.
Defosse, M. *Déontologie de la presse*, Presse de l'Université libre de Bruxelles, 1974.
Demarteau, Joseph, and Léon Duwaerts. *Droits et devoirs du journaliste*. Bruxelles:
    Maison de la presse, 1951.
Ferry, Jean-Marc. *Habermas, l'éthique de la communication*. Paris: PUF, 1987.
Friedman, Michel. *Libertés et responsabilités des journalistes et des auteurs*. Paris:
    CFPJ, 1989 (80 pages).
Halimi, Serge. *Les nouveaux chiens de garde*. Paris: Liber, 1997.
Kruuse, H., M. Berlins, and C. Grellier. *Les droits et les devoirs des journalistes dans
    les douze pays de l'Union Europeenne*. Paris: Centre de Formation et de
    Perfectionnement des Journalistes, 1994.
Libois, Boris. *Ethique de l'information: . Essai sur la déontologie journalistique*.
    Bruxelles: Ed. de l'Université, 1994.
Offler, M., and J-L. Hebarre. *Les organismes d'auto-contrôle de la presse à travers le
    monde*. Münich: C.H. Beck, 1968.
Pigeat, Henri. *Médias et déontologie*. Paris: PUF, 1997.
Pinto de Oliveira, C. J., and Bernard Neguin. *L'éthique professionnelle des journalistes*.
    Fribourg (Suisse): Editions universitaires, 1983.

Pinto de Oliveira, C. J. *Ethique de la communication sociale*. Fribourg: Editions universitaires, 1987.
Riboreau, Guy. *Déontologie du journalisme radiophonique*. Paris: RFI, 1997.
SNJ. *Livre blanc de la déontologie des journalistes ou de la pratique du métier au quotidien*. Paris: Syndicat national des journalistes, 1993.
Woodrow, Alain. *Information Manipulation*. Paris: Ed. du Félin, 1991.
Woodrow, Alain. *Les Médias: Quatrième pouvoir ou cinquième colonne?*. Paris: Editions du Félin, 1996.